D1308995

BOMBS OVER BIKINI

THE WORLD'S FIRST NUCLEAR DISASTER

CONNIE GOLDSMITH

TWENTY-FIRST CENTURY BOOKS / MINNEAPOLIS

*This book is dedicated to the people of the Marshall Islands,
whose lives were affected by the US nuclear testing program.*
—C.G.

Twenty-First Century Books
A division of Lerner Publishing Group, Inc.
241 First Avenue North
Minneapolis, MN 55401 USA

For reading levels and more information, look up this title at www.lernerbooks.com.

Library of Congress Cataloging-in-Publication Data

Goldsmith, Connie, 1945–
    Bombs over Bikini : the world's first nuclear disaster / by Connie Goldsmith.
    pages   cm
    Includes bibliographical references and index.
    ISBN 978–1–4677–1612–3 (lib. bdg. : alk. paper)
    ISBN 978–1–4677–2545–3 (ebook)
    1. Atomic bomb—Testing—Marshall Islands—Bikini Island. 2. Nuclear weapons—
Marshall Islands—Bikini Atoll—Testing. 3. Bikinians—Relocation—Marshall Islands.
4. Nuclear weapons testing victims—Marshall Islands—Bikini Atoll. 5. Nuclear weapons
testing victims—Marshall Islands—Rongelap Atoll. 6. Bikini Atoll (Marshall Islands)—
History. I. Title.
UG1282.A8.G63 2014
623.4'5119—dc23
                                                          2013017576

Manufactured in the United States of America
1 – DP – 12/31/13

CONTENTS

The US military detonated the world's first hydrogen bomb—*Bravo*—over a tiny atoll in the Marshall Islands on March 1, 1954. The explosion was part of a US nuclear testing program in the Marshall Islands in the Pacific Ocean. *Bravo*'s explosion *(above)* spread radiation across the region, contaminating islands, some of whose human populations had not been evacuated in preparation for the test bombing.

INTRODUCTION
TOXIC SNOWFALL

As soon as the war ended, we located the one spot on Earth that hadn't been touched by war and blew it to hell.

—BOB HOPE, US COMEDIAN, ACTOR, AND AUTHOR, 1947

March 1, 1954, was not a normal day on Rongelap Atoll in the Marshall Islands of the Pacific Ocean. That morning, the US military exploded the world's first hydrogen bomb—*Bravo*—on Nam, part of the Bikini Atoll about 75 miles (120 kilometers) away from Rongelap. Several hours later, white ash began to drift from the sky. It settled over the 236 people on Rongelap and Utrik (a small nearby atoll). The highly radioactive ash was the remnant of vaporized coral from Nam. "I began to feel a fine powder falling all over my body and into my eyes. The coconuts had changed color. By now all the trees were white, as well as my entire body. I didn't believe this was dangerous. The powder fell all day and night over the entire atoll of Rongelap," Mayor John Anjain later recalled.

No one on Rongelap knew what the powder was. More than an inch (2.5 centimeters) of it fell on the island. The radioactive powder drifted into food and houses. Some islanders who had been to the movies thought it was snow. Children played in it. People brushed the powder off their arms and legs, wiped it from their eyes, and spit it from their mouths. Within hours the Rongelap people fell ill with nausea, headaches and stomachaches, and irritated eyes and skin.

More than twenty-four hours after *Bravo*'s explosion, an American seaplane landed in the Rongelap lagoon. Two military officials came ashore carrying Geiger counters to measure radiation. The island's mayor and schoolteacher, both of whom spoke English and Marshallese, approached the men. Anjain asked why they had come to Rongelap. "They said they came to inspect the damage caused by the bomb. The men returned quickly to their plane and left. They probably didn't stay longer than ten minutes," Anjain said.

The Americans did not tell the men about the dangers of radiation. Instead, they left them—and all the inhabitants of Rongelap—where they were, covered in toxic fallout.

IN THE CONTEXT OF WAR

How did this happen? Why did the US military detonate an atomic bomb so close to an inhabited island? It began less than one year after the US military dropped the deadly atomic bombs over Hiroshima and Nagasaki, Japan, to end World War II (1939–1945). The US government then launched a new program. Called Operation Crossroads, the goal of this series of nuclear test bombings—to be set in the Marshall Islands—was to learn more about the effects of nuclear bombs and radiation on naval ships and animals. The military planned to detonate three bombs—one in the air and two in the water. *Able* was the first bomb of Operation Crossroads and was detonated over Bikini Atoll on July 1, 1946. Several other operations followed. *Bravo*, part of Operation Castle, came eight years later.

MANHATTAN PROJECT

In 1940 the United States suspected that Germany was working on a new type of bomb—an atomic bomb—that could produce an explosion bigger than any other existing technology. So in 1941, US president Franklin Roosevelt authorized the top secret Manhattan Engineering District—later called the Manhattan Project—to create an atomic bomb before the Germans could do so. Colonel Leslie Groves headed up the Manhattan Project. Dr. J. Robert Oppenheimer was the project's scientific director.

The Manhattan Project successfully developed the world's first atomic bomb, named *Trinity*, testing it in Alamogordo, New Mexico, on July 16, 1945. The United States dropped the world's second atomic bomb (*Little Boy*) on Hiroshima, Japan, on August 6, 1945, and the world's third atomic bomb (*Fat Man*) on Nagasaki, Japan, on August 9, 1945. Japan surrendered on August 15, 1945, ending World War II.

COUNTDOWN

Ten. Nine. Eight. Seven. Six. Five. Four. Three. Two. One. *"Bomb away, bomb away, bomb away and falling."* The crew of US bomber *Dave's Dream*, flying at 28,000 feet (8,534 meters) over the Pacific Ocean, released *Able*—the world's first peacetime atomic bomb. The B-29 Superfortress's 23,000-ton (23-kiloton) payload hit the target array, a collection of damaged and outdated warships at Bikini Atoll in the Marshall Islands. A swirling mushroom cloud of fire and gases rose more than 40,000 feet (12,192 m) into the air.

Radio stations around the world broadcast the detonation live. The blast was viewed from observation ships and planes by scientists; politicians; reporters; US military officials; and observers from several other countries, including China, Great Britain, and the Soviet Union (a union of fifteen republics that included Russia). *Able*'s explosion became the most photographed event up to that point in history. Scientists set up cameras atop towers on surrounding islands and on nearby observer ships. Radio-controlled drone airplanes flew over Bikini to photograph the blast. The US military had promised this and subsequent testing would develop important scientific knowledge with minimum risk to human life and livelihood. But the end result told a completely different story.

Employees at the Y-12 plant at Oak Ridge, Tennessee, change shifts during World War II. The Oak Ridge plant was one of the sites that developed uranium material for nuclear bombs as part of the Manhattan Project.

The pristine setting of Bikini Atoll was the site of the first test bomb of Operation Crossroads. Shortly before the US Navy evacuated islanders to Rongerik Atoll in preparation for the bombing, the community gathered for a final church service on Bikini in March 1946.

CHAPTER ONE

A GOOD PLACE FOR A BOMB

Would you be willing to sacrifice your island for the welfare of all men?

—COMMODORE BEN WYATT, US NAVY, TO BIKINI ISLANDERS, 1946

Halfway between Hawaii and Australia, the Marshall Islands stretch across a vast section of the Pacific Ocean. Some of the islands are so small and flat that the sea washes over them during storms. Others are big enough to hold a few small villages. The Marshalls are tropical islands, warm and humid most of the year. Breezes ruffle the coconut palms that sway over tangled greenery. White sand beaches circle sparkling lagoons. Fish flash through brilliant coral reefs. Turtles crawl ashore to lay their eggs. Crabs scuttle along the seafloor, and the occasional shark glides through the water looking for easy prey.

ISLANDS MADE OF SKELETONS

Millions of years ago, fiery volcanoes erupted at the bottom of the sea, eventually forming what are called the Marshall Islands. Corals—tiny living animals—grew on the uppermost section of the volcanoes, where they rose out of the water. Over thousands of years, the volcanoes sank back into the sea. But the corals continued to grow, seeking sunlight at the ocean's surface. Finally, all that remained of the ancient volcanoes were a series of lagoons, each surrounded by a ring of coral islands called an atoll.

FORMATION OF AN ATOLL

The animals that form a coral reef are called coral polyps. Each one is smaller than a pencil eraser. Colonies of polyps secrete a mineral called calcium carbonate, which forms an external skeleton. When old polyps die, new polyps grow on the hard surface of the dead ones and produce more calcium carbonate. The skeletons of trillions of coral polyps heaped one atop the other formed the atolls of the Marshall Islands. As centuries passed, waves and rain broke down the coral into white sand beaches. Wind and water carried dust from faraway islands and deposited it on the shoreline, where it formed soil.

SETTLING THE ISLANDS

About two thousand years ago, people first came to the Marshalls. They paddled from other Pacific islands in outrigger canoes to look for new homes. For centuries Marshallese women cared for children and prepared food for their families, while men fished, gathered crops, and built outrigger canoes from the wood of breadfruit trees. The islands provided everything people needed. Although the Marshall Islands were remote, explorers from several nations visited them over the centuries. A Spanish explorer reached the islands in 1529. English captain John Marshall visited the islands in 1788 and named them after himself. Religious missionaries from New England arrived in the 1850s and converted many of the islanders to Christianity.

Japan seized control of the Marshall Islands from Germany in 1914 during World War I (1914–1918). The Japanese established a weather station on Bikini Atoll and built large military bases on Kwajalein and Enewetak Atolls. They treated the Marshallese harshly, forcing the islanders to build the military fortifications. They also forced the local children to go to Japanese schools, where they required children to learn math and the Japanese language. Students dared not be late for school. "If we didn't come to school on time, the soldiers would put us to work for the day with the men, digging holes for water wells or making latrines for the soldiers," remembered Biamon Lewis, a Bikinian who lived under Japanese rule.

The Japanese ruled Bikini for about thirty years until World War II reached the islands. In 1944, toward the end of the war, the United States defeated Japan in fierce battles on Kwajalein and Enewetak. These two atolls became US bases. Americans introduced a new prosperity to the islands. They brought doctors, who provided free medical care, as well as food and supplies that had been difficult to obtain under the Japanese. With these supplies, the islanders were better able to keep their outrigger canoes in good working order. During the war, Bikini had been cut off from other islands and unable to trade copra (dried coconut meat). After the arrival of the Americans, the Bikinians were once more able to make and trade copra. The Marshallese used money from copra sales to buy processed and manufactured goods such as rice, flour, sugar, tea, coffee, kerosene lamps, cooking utensils, fish hooks, and clothing.

"ACCEPTABLE RISK AND MINIMUM HAZARD"

World War II ended in August 1945 when the United States dropped atomic bombs on the Japanese cities of Hiroshima and Nagasaki. The bombs flattened huge portions of both cities and instantly killed an estimated 120,000 people. Thousands more died later from radiation injuries. After the war, the United States and its former ally, the Soviet Union, emerged as the world's main superpowers. For decades the two nations faced off in a chilling military and political competition known as the Cold War (1945–1991). Each nation worked feverishly to outpace the other in scientific and military achievements, including the development of powerful nuclear arsenals.

The atomic bomb was a completely new weapon at the time, and scientists wanted to learn more about the bomb's capacity. In particular, Americans wanted to know if nuclear bombs could sink large naval ships. Admiral William H. P. Blandy explained that the US Navy wanted "to determine the effect of the atom bomb against various types of naval vessels. With the information, we can improve our ship design, tactics, and strategy, to minimize our losses in the unfortunate event of war waged with atomic weapons." He also underscored the larger political considerations, saying, "It is essential that no country gain ascendancy over the United States in the development, manufacture, and tactical use of atomic weapons." So US president Harry Truman ordered military officials to select a place to carry out nuclear testing. President Truman said the site had to "permit accomplishment of the tests with acceptable risk and minimum hazard."

The ideal site for the tests would be under US control. The winds would have to be predictable to better control nuclear fallout (radiation), and the climate had to be mild to allow personnel to work without fear of disruptive storms. A large sheltered lagoon would be the perfect setting to anchor target ships. And because B-29s were the only planes big enough to carry atomic bombs, the site would have to be located within 1,000 miles (1,600 km) of a B-29 base.

Military planners also thought about human considerations. For example, Admiral Blandy—who would be the naval commander in charge of the testing program—said, "It was important that the local population [of the test site] be small and cooperative so they could be moved to a new location with a minimum of trouble." And the site had to be far away from the United States to protect Americans from the radioactive fallout of the testing.

Military officials unfolded their world maps and started searching. They looked at islands in the Caribbean Sea and in the Atlantic and Pacific Oceans. In January 1946, Admiral Blandy announced to a congressional committee that he had found the perfect site: the Bikini Atoll in the Marshall Islands. And he told the committee that he had named the atomic bomb testing program Operation Crossroads. "Sea power, airpower, and perhaps humanity itself are at the crossroads," he said.

LET'S MEET AFTER CHURCH

By 1946 US military officials had been visiting Bikini—under US control after the war—for nearly two years. Military officials visited every few months to bring food, supplies, and doctors. The Americans built a school and a medical clinic staffed by navy-trained medics. The Americans provided for many of the Bikinians' needs and introduced a new form of community government. The Bikinians thought well of the Americans, adopting them as their *irioj alap*—their highest chief. According to Marshallese tradition, the high chief status meant the Americans were responsible for the islanders' protection and welfare. The Bikinians were unlikely to turn down any request the Americans made.

Sundays on Bikini were entirely devoted to worship. The Bikinians attended church services, where they listened to their pastor's sermon and sang hymns enlivened with island rhythms. On Sunday, February 10, 1946, Commodore Ben Wyatt of the US Navy invited the island's 167 inhabitants to meet with him after church. The islanders sat cross-legged in a semicircle under the coconut palms, waiting to hear what the American had to say. Wyatt had arrived the day before on a seaplane along with other military men, a photographer, and a Marshallese translator. "It was an historic occasion," the navy reported, "this impact of the accumulated scientific knowledge of centuries upon a primitive people."

Commodore Wyatt described the power of the atomic bomb

American naval commander Ben Wyatt *(far left)* met with the residents of Bikini in February 1946 to persuade them to leave their island home in preparation for the test launch of *Able*. He appealed to religious and humanitarian sentiments to sway the islanders, who in the end would never be able to return home.

and how it had destroyed Hiroshima and Nagasaki. He said the Americans wanted to learn how to use the bomb for the good of mankind and to end all wars. To do so, he explained that the US military wanted to use Bikini Atoll as the site of its testing program. The Bikini population would be asked to leave the island for safety's sake. In making his pitch, Wyatt purposely made a religious appeal to gain approval of the plan. He drew upon the Bible, a book the Bikinians knew well. He compared them to the children of Israel whom God had led into the Promised Land.

Wyatt had chosen his moment well. His was an argument the Bikinians found hard to resist. Chief Juda reached a decision for his community later that day. "If the United States and the scientists of the world want to use our island and atoll, which with God's blessing will result in benefit to all mankind, my people will be pleased to go elsewhere."

MOVING OUT, MOVING IN

After a few days of discussion, the Bikinians agreed to move to Rongerik, an uninhabited atoll 125 miles (200 km) from Bikini. "We were a very close-knit group of people back then. We were like one big happy family. After we made the final decision [to leave Bikini] no one had any problems with it. We agreed to go along with whatever was decided by our leaders," Bikinian Emso Leviticus said. Commodore Wyatt had told the Bikinians that the move would be temporary and that the islanders could return to Bikini in a few months. At the time, little was known about the lingering effects of radiation in the environment, so the Bikinians believed Wyatt's assessment.

Rongerik is near Rongelap, an atoll the Bikinians often visited. While Rongerik was not ideal, the people preferred to move to the uninhabited atoll so they wouldn't be subject to the rule of the leader of another island. Navy officials told US reporters that Rongerik had more trees, that it was richer in food supplies, and that the coconuts were bigger there. In reality, Rongerik was

Bikini islanders evacuated their homeland on March 7, 1946, four months before the first of the Operation Crossroads nuclear weapons tests.

much smaller than Bikini and had far fewer resources.

The US Navy gave the Bikinians less than a month to prepare for the move from their ancestral atoll. One night the navy treated the islanders to movies on the deck of the USS *Sumner*, a navy survey ship. The children had never seen movies before. They giggled at Mickey Mouse cartoons and enjoyed a western. On March 6, 1946, the day before the evacuation, the Bikinians visited their cemetery and decorated the graves with flowers and coconut fronds. They prayed and said good-bye to their ancestors.

The next morning, March 7, 1946, the islanders boarded a Landing Ship, Tank (an LST, a landing boat to carry people and cargo between a ship and a beach) with their boxes, bundles, and chickens. A crane lifted outrigger canoes and stowed them on deck. The navy had already transported tents, building supplies, and an American flag to Rongerik in preparation for the move. The trip from Bikini Atoll to Rongerik Atoll took one day. Two days later, on March 10, 1946, naval officials raised the American flag over the island. They left the Bikinians alone on Rongerik with fresh water and a month's supply of food.

In the context of the Cold War arms race, Operation Crossroads was viewed as a necessary effort to keep up with the Soviets. The US Post Office issued a commemorative envelope *(above)* in July 1946 to mark the first of the Bikini Atoll test bombings.

CHAPTER TWO

ABLE:
THE FIRST BOMB

The Atomic Age is here. The atomic bomb is the most lethal destructive agent yet devised by man. Its energy release is staggering; its radioactivity is slow killing poison.

—ADMIRAL WILLIAM H. P. BLANDY, 1946

Operation Crossroads was one of the biggest military operations of its time, with a budget of $1.3 billion. The plan was to detonate three atomic bombs. *Able* would be released in the air, and *Baker* would be detonated underwater. (The third bomb, *Charlie*, was later canceled.) As the project got off the ground in February 1946, nearly forty-two thousand military and civilian personnel worked in and around Bikini, Kwajalein, and Enewetak Atolls to prepare the test site and to build housing for workers. The food preparation alone was astounding. Personnel ate 38,000 pounds (17,236 kilograms) of fruit, 40,000 pounds (18,144 kg) of meat, 89,000 pounds (40,370 kg) of vegetables, and seventy thousand candy bars *each day*.

Navy workers built laboratories, dormitories, lunchrooms, clinics, and recreational facilities for the huge number of people working in the area. They set up the first radio station in the Marshall Islands, calling it Radio Bikini. Four newspapers informed everyone about the complex preparations for the atomic bomb tests.

Workmen blasted large holes through the fragile coral reef encircling Bikini Atoll so ships could enter the otherwise enclosed lagoon. The navy then sailed or towed nearly one hundred ships into the lagoon and anchored them to serve as targets for the bombs. The ships included German and Japanese ships captured in the war as well as US ships too outdated or damaged to be of further use.

As launch day, July 1, 1946, neared, plans shifted into high gear. Pilots flew B-29 Superfortress bombers from Kwajalein, dropping fake bombs called pumpkins over the target array for practice. Four B-29 crews competed to be chosen to carry the real bomb, known as *Able*, aboard *Dave's Dream*. Military officials selected Major Woodrow Swancutt from Wisconsin to pilot the plane that would carry *Able*. Major Harold Wood of New Jersey would be the bombardier, the man responsible for sighting and releasing the bomb. Between the two of them, the men had flown more than seventy bombing missions during World War II.

WOODROW P. SWANCUTT

Woodrow Paul Swancutt, nicknamed Woody, was born in Wisconsin in 1915. He graduated from high school in 1933 and attended the University of Wisconsin at Madison. In college he was a member of the Wisconsin Badgers boxing team and was the national intercollegiate middleweight boxing champion.

Swancutt had planned to be a doctor but left his premedical studies to enter the US Air Force in November 1940 as an aviation cadet. He served as a B-29 pilot and flew forty-nine combat missions in the Far East and Pacific during World War II. He flew the first daylight B-29 attack on Japan against the Yawata Steel Works, an especially dangerous mission.

After Operation Crossroads, Swancutt served at air force bases in several states and in England. He held a number of high positions during his distinguished military career and reached the position of major general and of vice commander of the Second Air Force. He retired in 1968.

Swancutt logged more than eight thousand flying hours. His decorations included the Legion of Merit with two oak leaf clusters, the Distinguished Flying Cross and Air Medal with oak leaf clusters, and the Air Force Commendation Medal. He is buried at Arlington National Cemetery, in Arlington, Virginia.

JULY 1, 1946

Just after midnight, in a hanger on Kwajalein, a crane hoisted *Able* into the bomb bay of *Dave's Dream*. The crew had given *Able* the nickname *Gilda*, after a movie character played by popular Hollywood star Rita Hayworth. At 3:20 a.m., Swancutt and his crew sat down to breakfast in the mess hall. Dense clouds hung over Bikini. It looked as if the test might be canceled. But over the next two hours, the clouds drifted away. At 5:42 a.m., Admiral Blandy gave the go-ahead.

Swancutt jumped into a jeep and sped across the tarmac to prepare for takeoff. His crew joined him as he boarded the B-29. At 5:53 a.m., Swancutt revved up the B-29's four engines. Two weapons specialists, crouched inside the bomb bay, flipped the switches that prepared the bomb for detonation as the plane readied for takeoff.

Woodrow Swancutt *(left)* piloted *Dave's Dream*, the bomber that released *Able* over Bikini Atoll in 1946. The plane was a B-29, a four-engine propeller-driven heavy bomber designed by Boeing, which manufactured hundreds of planes each month for the US military during World War II.

Politicians, international leaders, and members of the international press arrived to observe the test. To photograph the event, scientists and military officials set up hundreds of cameras. They placed them on unmanned drone planes that would fly over *Able* itself, on land-based towers, on nearby observation ships, and on some of the ships of the target array itself. Nearly half the world's supply of film was used at Bikini to shoot fifty thousand photographs and 284 miles (457 km) of movie film.

As *Dave's Dream* began its taxi down the runway shortly before 6:00 a.m., radio newsman Bill Chaplin spoke into his microphone from the observation post above the tarmac. "Now the plane is swinging around. He's giving her the gun! The atom bomb plane, *Dave's Dream* is starting down the runway. Fifty miles [80 km] an hour, now sixty [97 km] . . . He's up! The plane is airborne. The atom bomb is in the air on its way to Bikini for the greatest experiment in history," the excited reporter shouted.

Dozens of observer and drone planes were already in the air. The observer planes would cruise at a safe distance from the bomb to view the explosion and film it. Drone planes controlled by radio signals were to fly directly over the explosion to take close-up photos and measure radiation.

At 8:30 a.m., Swancutt made a run over the Bikini Lagoon to spot his target, the US battleship *Nevada*. The navy had painted it red so it would be easy to see from the air. A metronome on the target ship USS *Pennsylvania* ticked out the countdown on worldwide radio. "It came to sound like a voice of doom tolling the world's last minutes," reporter William Laurence said. "When the metronome stops, the atomic bomb has exploded."

"Two minutes to go," Wood announced over his radio from *Dave's Dream*. "Release minus two minutes." The bomber, guided by a radar beacon, flew at 28,000 feet (8,534 m) and soon only seconds remained. "Ten. Nine. Eight. Seven. Six. Five. Four. Three. Two. One. Mark! Bomb away, bomb away, bomb away and falling."

The metronome fell silent.

Photographers and other official observers on the USS *Mount McKinley* record the mushroom cloud that rose into the air just seconds after *Able* detonated.

Wood released *Able* just before 9:00 a.m. The bomb exploded 518 feet (158 m) above the lagoon. A huge ball of fire shot high into the air, reaching a temperature of 100,000°F (55,538°C), hotter than the surface of the sun. Swirling masses of flaming red, purple, and white clouds erupted from the lagoon. A mushroom-shaped cloud boiled up from the ball of fire, rising more than 40,000 feet (12,192 m) into the sky within just a few minutes.

"When the flash came it lighted up sky and ocean with the light of many suns, a light not of the earth," reporter Bill Laurence said. Journalist Gerald Gross reported, "We saw a giant column rising into the substratosphere like a genie out of a diabolic thousand and one nights [referring to the *Arabian Nights* folktales], creamy white inside and surrounded by a crimson glow."

Manned planes flew over the target array to check the ships for visible damage. Drone planes moved closer to take samples from the mushroom cloud. Remote-controlled drone boats measured the water in the lagoon for radioactivity. Much of the radiation had been swept up high into the stratosphere and dispersed over a huge area. The navy called *Able* a "self-cleansing" bomb, claiming that the spread of radiation into the stratosphere had cleared out most of the radiation from Bikini.

Less than six hours after the explosion, Blandy gave the all-clear. Blandy was satisfied with *Able*'s performance. "The bomb was dropped with very good accuracy. I am very pleased with the excellent performance of our task force in the operation. It could not have been better."

ABLE'S ANIMALS

A month before the detonation of *Able*, the US Navy had deployed the USS *Burleson*, nicknamed *Noah's Ark*, to Bikini. The ship held 146 pigs, 176 goats, 57 guinea pigs, and 3,139 rodents. All the animals were to be part of the test, to learn more about the effects of radioactive fallout on living creatures. Each animal was tattooed with an identifying number, and seamen and veterinarians cared for the animals until the launch day.

At first, Blandy denied animals would be used in the testing. He later reversed himself, publicly stating that "a minimum number of animals will be used. We regret some of these animals may be sacrificed, but we are more concerned about the men and women of the next generation than we are about the animals of this one."

Animal lovers around the world protested the use of animals, calling the plan cruel and barbarous. Dogs were originally part of the test group, but dog lovers protested so loudly that Blandy decided to exclude dogs. Seven hundred people volunteered to serve

Seaman Second Class Dale Lipps *(left)* and Seaman Second Class Richard M. Williamson *(right)* arrive in the United States with Pig 311 and Goat BO Plenty three months after the *Able* explosion. Both animals were exposed to radioactive fallout as part of the weapons testing experiment.

as human guinea pigs instead of the animals. General Thomas J. Betts declined these offers, telling reporters at a press conference that "some [of the volunteers] are obviously cranks. Some people are daredevils. Some of them want a little publicity. We try to be courteous to them."

In preparation for launch day, sailors placed the animals on twenty-two of the target ships at duty stations that humans would typically occupy in battle: decks and bridges, gun turrets and engine rooms, and halyards (ropes for hoisting and lowering flags, adders, and other equipment). Some goats were shaved to mimic military buzz cuts to see if the explosion or radiation would affect military personnel, who typically wear their hair very short. Other animals were covered with sunblock to determine if sunblock protected against the flash of the explosion. Pigs, whose skin is similar to human skin, were smeared with antiflash lotion to see if it would protect them from harmful radiation. A few pigs were dressed in navy uniforms to discover if fabric offered any protection against radiation. An Operations Crossroad press release clarified, "It is not the intention to kill a large portion of the animals since dead animals are of less value for study. We want radiation-sick animals, not radiation-dead animals."

Even so, about one-fourth of the animals died during the explosion. Onboard cameras showed that some of the animals

PIG 311

Many animals died as a result of the *Able* explosion. But one animal survived without a scratch. Animal 311 was a young pig locked in a bathroom on the Japanese cruiser *Sakawa*, part of the target fleet moored in the Bikini Lagoon. The blast set the *Sakawa* on fire, but the ship didn't sink until the next day. American sailors found Pig 311 swimming in the Bikini Lagoon several hours after the *Sakawa* sank. They sent Pig 311 to the Naval Medical Research Institute in Maryland for examination. Other than a foul temper and a low blood count, the pig seemed normal and recovered fully. She ended her days at a zoo in Washington, DC, where she grew from a 50-pound (23 kg) piglet to a 600-pound (272 kg) porker.

were amazingly resilient, however. Goats tethered on open decks munched hay during the explosion and throughout the shipboard fires that followed. A rat gave birth to three babies as the bomb went off. Sailors named them Alpha, Beta, and Gamma, after three types of radiation. Over the next few months, however, most of the animals died from radiation damage to their bone marrow, the soft material inside bones where blood cells are formed.

Animals Used in Bikini A-Bomb Test Reported to Be 'Dying Like Flies'

KWAJALEIN, July 15 (Monday.) (*P*)—A report that Bikini test animals have begun "dying like flies" came today from the U.S.S. Burleson, highly-secret animal ship from which reporters have been barred.

An officer who visited the Burleson said animals that appear healthy and have a normal blood count one day "drop off the next day."

Asked whether any animals would be taken to the United States for further study, as originally planned, the officer exclaimed:

"What animals?"

The inference was that at the rate the animals were dying recently there soon would be few if any left.

Another officer said that the amazing Pig 311, fished from the waters of Bikini Lagoon after the July 1 atomic bomb explosion, still was alive yesterday.

He understood, however, that Pig 311 was showing a diminishing blood count and other internal signs of damage.

At the indicated rate the animals are dying, it now seems fairly certain the atomic bomb radioactivity at Bikini was far more deadly than many had thought.

One captain, after studying conditions aboard his target ship, estimated personnel loss would have been 70 per cent had it been manned.

An article in the *Los Angeles Times* on July 15, 1946, shortly after the *Able* explosion, reported on the death of test animals, pointing specifically to the high level of radioactivity released at Bikini Atoll.

Baker was detonated 90 feet (27 m) underwater, releasing a cloud of visible water vapor known as a Wilson cloud, or a condensation cloud. The cloud appears when nuclear explosives or large amounts of conventional explosives are detonated in very humid air.

CHAPTER THREE

BAKER:
THE WATER BOMB

The phenomenon was one of the most spectacular and awe-inspiring sights ever seen by man on this planet.

—WILLIAM L. LAURENCE, *NEW YORK TIMES* JOURNALIST, 1946

nlike *Able*, which had been detonated in the air, *Baker* would be detonated underwater. Numerous cameras and drone planes would be in place to capture the events on film, and print journalists were on-site to record their observations.

Experts had warned Admiral Blandy that such an explosion would be dangerous. The explosion—planned for July 25, 1946—would not spit the radiation into the atmosphere where it could be swept away by winds. Instead, radiation would be contained in the water, contaminating the target ships, the lagoon, and Bikini Island. Radioactive water could drift thousands of miles across shipping lanes or inhabited islands.

Scientists and the military debated. In the end, Blandy ordered his men to explode *Baker* underwater. So seamen placed the bomb in a concrete chamber and hung it beneath the USS *LSM-60*, an amphibious assault ship anchored in the lagoon at Bikini.

AN UNEXPECTED VISITOR

Two days before the test, Chief Juda flew to Bikini in Commodore Wyatt's seaplane. His arrival came as a surprise. Although Blandy had invited the chief to watch the *Baker* explosion, he apparently didn't believe Chief Juda would attend. Officers scrambled to welcome Chief Juda to the USS *Mount McKinley*, where naval officials would be watching the detonation of the bomb. Chief Juda saluted them as he boarded.

In kindergarten vocabulary, an interpreter described the upcoming explosion to Chief Juda. "The bomb will blow much water up in air, way up, much water, high." Chief Juda nodded his understanding, saying that he hoped to bring his people back to their homes on Bikini after the tests.

A TERROR-INSPIRING SIGHT

The ships that had survived *Able* served as target array for *Baker*. On launch day, Marshall Holloway waited in the control room aboard the USS *Cumberland Sound* 15 miles (24 km) from the target site. Holloway was a scientist who had helped develop the

WILLIAM H. P. BLANDY

William Henry Purnell Blandy had a distinguished navy career spanning thirty-seven years, from 1913 to 1950. Born in New York City in 1890, he graduated first in his class from the US Naval Academy in 1913. He served his country during both World War I and World War II.

In World War II, Admiral Blandy was a commander in the Pacific and participated in the battle for Iwo Jima in 1945. After World War II, he commanded the navy task force responsible for the atomic bomb tests at Bikini Atoll. He later served as commander in chief, Atlantic Fleet. Blandy retired in 1950. He died at the US Naval Hospital in Saint Albans, New York, at the age of sixty-three. He is buried at Arlington National Cemetery.

world's first atomic bomb as part of the Manhattan Project. He sat at an electronic control panel whose rows of buttons would control *Baker*'s firing sequence. At 8:35 a.m., Holloway began pushing the buttons one by one, setting the automatic bomb-firing clock in motion. After the last button, a radio signal triggered the detonation.

"A gigantic dome of water, white, beautiful, terror-inspiring, at least a mile [1.6 km] wide, rose nearly a mile in the air," wrote Philip Porter, reporter for the *Cleveland Plain Dealer* newspaper. Steven White, of the *New York Herald Tribune*, said the explosion was "so fantastic, so mighty and so beyond belief that men's emotions burst from their throats in wild shouts."

Scientists were more precise in their descriptions. Within a few millionths of a second, the explosion formed an underwater fireball bubble. It generated a powerful shock wave that moved faster than the speed of sound, about 761 miles (1,225 km) per hour. The shock wave dug a giant crater in the floor of the lagoon about 200 feet (61 m) below the surface of the water. Above the surface, a dome of seawater erupted like a giant geyser.

One second after the explosion, the expanding fireball bubble threw 2.2 million tons (2 million metric tons) of water, sand, and pulverized coral into the air. The bubble boiled up into a hollow column of water more than a mile (1.6 km) high. The intense heat of the bubble caused water in the humid tropical air to condense, producing what scientists call a Wilson condensation cloud. The cloud hid the water column for a few seconds before it flattened into a doughnut shape and vanished. The hollow column of water and debris came back into view and climbed to about 10,000 feet (3,048 m). At that altitude, it became a cauliflower-shaped cloud, quite distinct from the well-known mushroom cloud of previous atomic explosions.

Eleven seconds after the explosion, lagoon water rushed into the empty space left by the rising fireball bubble, starting a series of tsunami-like waves. The first wave was 94 feet (29 m) high. By the time the waves reached Bikini Island, they had leveled out. A series of 15-foot (4.6 m) waves rolled over the flat island, temporarily submerging it.

Twelve seconds after the blast, water from the column created a 900-foot (274 m) base surge, similar to the dense mist at the bottom of a huge waterfall. Most of the bomb's radiation fell into the base surge, contaminating the water. The huge wall of spray and debris rapidly billowed outward, drifting 7 miles (11 km) and rolling over all the target vessels.

CONTAMINATED!

As scientists had predicted, the radiation from *Baker* did not disperse into the atmosphere. Instead, massive amounts of radioactive material fell back into Bikini Lagoon and onto the target vessels anchored there. The amount of radiation on target ships immediately after the blast was twenty times greater than that of a fatal dose. Yet only forty minutes later, patrol boats entered the lagoon to examine the damaged vessels.

The navy claimed it had protected servicemen from radiation, yet some observer ships and their crew were caught in the fallout. The 1988 documentary film *Radio Bikini* shows sailors wearing little or no protection as they inspect the target ships shortly after the explosion.

A US Navy crew swabs the decks of the *Prinz Eugen*, a German warship that was part of the *Baker* target array, in an effort to wash away the radioactive fallout with which the ship was drenched. The crew did the job with no protective gear whatsoever.

Two hours later, technicians briefly boarded the highly radioactive ships to retrieve test instruments. Seaman John Smitherman, stationed on the USS *Sumner*, later recalled, "We didn't know what was going on. No one told us anything about radiation. We were caught in what they called the downwind. A lot of debris fell on the *Sumner*: mist, grit, sand and pieces of rock. I picked up a little rock and put it in my pocket."

By the end of the day, fifteen thousand military officials, sailors, and scientists on forty-nine support ships had entered the lagoon to carry out post-detonation testing. Smitherman recalled, "We saw men coming on board with Geiger counters and they were walking all over the ship. They had regular shoes on with paper over them. I had on a pair of shorts and tennis shoes and a little T-shirt and a sailor hat. We were swimming in the water and there was a lot of dead fish around. Water was pulled into the ship to make our drinking water. We used the water to wash our clothes with. They continued to tell us to not worry. We wasn't [sic] in any danger whatsoever."

But in fact, the men were in danger. The seawater and the vessels were highly contaminated. Nonetheless, for two months, sailors tried to decontaminate the target ships without any type of protection. For example, sailors scrubbed the decks with water, soap, and lye using mops and brushes. They used giant fire hoses to spray seawater over the decks, trying to wash off the radioactivity. But the water was even more radioactive than the ships, and mops and brushes simply spread the radiation.

The support ships moved in and out of the lagoon, depending on the day's radiation readings. Yet the Geiger counters were unable to measure every form of radiation that the bomb produced. In addition, the salt air and high humidity caused many Geiger counters to malfunction. Scientists and navy officials argued back and forth about safety. Navy officials wanted decontamination work to continue. Scientists felt the military was downplaying the dangers.

The navy finally halted attempts to decontaminate the target vessels in the lagoon, realizing it was a nearly impossible job. Some of them were towed to Kwajalein and scuttled. Less contaminated vessels were taken back to shipyards in the United States, where they were decontaminated and removed from commission. Many were left to rest at the bottom of the lagoon. By the end of September 1946, all Operation Crossroads personnel had left Bikini Atoll. What had once been a much-loved home to the Bikinians was now a nightmarish radioactive junkyard of broken ships and equipment left to rust on filthy beaches.

THE REAL COSTS OF CROSSROADS

How dangerous was Operation Crossroads? Seaman John Smitherman—who had walked on contaminated decks wearing only tennis shoes—developed serious burns on his feet and legs one month after *Baker*. He lost both his legs to amputation after radiation caused severe, irreversible swelling. He died thirty-seven years after *Baker* from cancer of the lungs, liver, and colon.

Atomic veteran Seaman John Smitherman (*left*, shortly before his death) watched the *Baker* explosion from a ship that was about 20 miles (32 km) from the blast. He later developed severe swelling (*see his hand in the photo at left*) related to blockage of the lymph system and had both legs amputated. He died in 1983 from cancer of the colon, liver, and lungs.

As years passed, veterans of Operation Crossroads and their families argued that exposure to radiation had caused their cancers. Yet cancer is a common disease, causing nearly one-fourth of all deaths in the United States. When cancer develops many years after exposure to radiation, it is difficult to know for certain if radiation caused it. Nonetheless, radiation dangers from *Baker* were poorly managed. The navy's own records admitted to an unexpectedly massive amount of radioactive contamination. There were too few radiation officers and radiation badges (devices penned to clothing that track how much radiation people receive) to protect the men. The level of radiation deemed safe at that time was 0.1 roentgens (a measure of radiation) *per day*. In the twenty-first century, 0.1 roentgens is the recommended exposure *per year*. Overall, Operation Crossroads officials, from the top officers to the youngest sailors, did not understand the dangers of radiation or downplayed it.

Navy admiral William H. P. Blandy *(far left)* and his wife cut a cake in the shape of a nuclear mushroom cloud at a 1946 reception celebrating Operation Crossroads. Most people involved in the test program felt they were participating in a valuable effort to modernize the US military in a time of intense military competition with the Soviets. At the time, the US military felt the risks to human life were worth taking.

In 1996 a US government-sponsored study looked at medical records of twelve thousand veterans of Operation Crossroads. On average, they lived three months less than military personnel who had not been a part of Crossroads. The study found Crossroads veterans had a 4.6 percent greater risk of premature death than did nonveterans. The men who boarded the target ships after *Baker* had a 5.7 percent increased risk.

CANCELING *CHARLIE*

After *Baker* the US Navy planned to detonate another underwater bomb, called *Charlie*, 1 mile (1.6 km) underwater in 1947. But scientists felt the test would have no scientific value. *Baker* had answered all the questions about underwater atomic explosions, they said. In addition, Bikini Island and its lagoon were so highly radioactive that measuring a third bomb's radiation in the same location could not be accurate. So the navy canceled that test.

However, nuclear testing in the Marshall Islands resumed in 1948. Between 1946 and 1958, the United States detonated sixty-seven nuclear bombs at Bikini and at Enewetak Atoll about 190 miles (305 km) from Bikini. Bombs fell from the air, bombs rested on barges, and bombs dangled from ships and hot-air balloons. But *Bravo*, bomb number 12, sometimes called the world's first nuclear disaster, was the most infamous bomb of all.

At a March 19, 1954, news conference in Tokyo, Japan, doctors point to radiation burns suffered by two Japanese fishermen covered by radioactive fallout from the *Bravo* explosion on March 1. With its history of human suffering from American nuclear bombings, the Japanese were particularly outraged by the test program and its devastating impact on human life.

CHAPTER FOUR

BRAVO:
THE BIG BOMB

Bravo had an explosive force of 1.5 million tons [1.4 million metric tons] of TNT [dynamite]. A freight train carrying the bomb's equivalent in TNT would span the United States from Maine to California.

—JONATHAN M. WEISGALL, ATTORNEY AND BIKINI ADVOCATE, 1994

From space, Rongelap Atoll looks like a puzzle piece waiting to be slipped into the blue and white jigsaw of the Pacific Ocean. Sixty-one small coral islands make up the atoll, which lies 100 miles (161 km) east of Bikini. The people of the Bikini and Rongelap Atolls had known each other for centuries and often married into one another's families. And like Bikini Atoll, Rongelap Atoll had been a peaceful home to its inhabitants for two thousand years. That changed on March 1, 1954, when the world's first nuclear disaster changed their lives forever.

FISSION VS. FUSION

After the *Able* and *Baker* test bombings, the United States exploded more atomic bombs in the Marshall Islands: three in 1948, four in 1951, and two in 1952. The twelfth bomb was called *Bravo*. It was part of Operation Castle, a series of explosions intended to test a new kind of bomb. While *Able* and *Baker* were fission bombs, *Bravo* was a fusion bomb.

Fission

fissionable nucleus

fission product
(radioactive
nucleus)

fissionable
nuclei
(three shown)

nucleus
splitting

energy
release

fission product
(radioactive
nucleus)

chain
reaction

Fission and fusion bombs differ greatly. All matter is composed of atoms. Each atom contains a nucleus made of protons, which have a positive electrical charge, and neutrons, which have no electrical charge. A powerful force holds the nucleus together. Electrons, which have a negative charge, circle the nucleus like tiny planets orbiting a sun. Fission bombs explode when neutrons hit the nucleus of an atom of a heavy element such as uranium. The neutrons split the uranium into lighter elements. More neutrons bombard other nuclei of other atoms and so on, triggering a chain reaction. These bombs are called atomic bombs, or A-bombs.

Fusion bombs release energy when the nuclei of atoms of lighter-weight elements such as hydrogen or helium combine to

Fusion

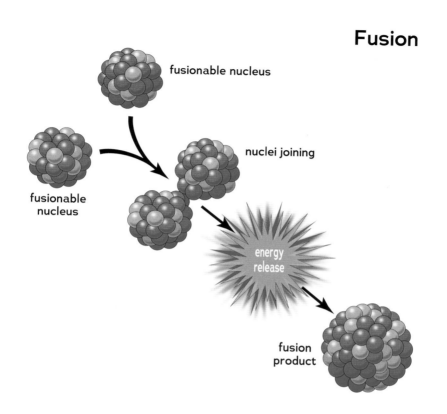

fusionable nucleus

nuclei joining

fusionable
nucleus

energy
release

fusion
product

form heavier elements. These bombs are called hydrogen bombs,
or H-bombs. Fusion bombs are much more powerful than fission
bombs.

The United States had tested its first H-bomb, called *Mike,* on
Enewetak in 1952. *Mike* detonated successfully, but it was not a
deliverable bomb. Bigger than a two-story house, it was too big to be
carried in a plane in the event of war.

BRAVO

At this point, the United States was ahead of the Soviet Union in
the Cold War arms race. But it didn't take long for the Soviet Union
to catch up with the Americans. The Soviets set off the world's

first deliverable H-bomb in 1953. US president Dwight Eisenhower could not let the Soviets surge ahead. The United States needed a deliverable hydrogen bomb—and quickly.

By 1954 a deliverable H-bomb was ready to be tested. Code-named *Bravo*, it was the first test in the Operation Castle program. Early in 1954, a US naval ship and its crew of sailors and scientists carried *Bravo* to the Marshall Islands. Destroyers flanked the ship. Planes circled overhead to protect it from the air. The convoy sailed at night, with lights turned off and radios silenced. The ships avoided regular shipping lanes as another means to prevent detection.

Scientists placed *Bravo* on a sandbar near tiny Nam Island at the edge of Bikini Atoll. The bomb rested inside a giant steel container with a door at one end. The bomb itself was only 5 feet (1.5 m) wide and 20 feet (6 m) long, small enough to deliver by plane.

US officials had decided not to evacuate nearby Rongelap prior to the detonation of *Bravo* even though they had done so with previous bomb tests. In fact, the United States did not even notify the islanders that a test was scheduled.

Before the explosion, US military weathermen monitored the weather in an area of the Pacific as large as the United States. At lower altitudes, the winds over Bikini Island were blowing toward the west, so scientists expected the wind would blow the radiation westward away from inhabited islands and out into the open ocean. The night before the *Bravo* test, weather reports showed wind conditions worsening. Shortly before the blast, winds at 20,000 feet (6,100 m) were, in fact, blowing eastward, toward Rongelap.

"The wind had been blowing straight at us for days," said Gene Curbow, senior weatherman on Rongerik Atoll, about 135 miles (217 km) east of Bikini, in an interview with the *New York Times* newspaper in 1982. "It was blowing straight at us during the test and straight at us after it. The wind never shifted." Dr. Alvin Graves, scientific director of Operation Castle, had final authority over whether the test would proceed. He decided to fire *Bravo* even though it seemed certain the winds would carry toxic fallout to Rongelap and its inhabitants.

On the morning of March 1, 1954, nine American scientists gathered in a heavily protected concrete bunker about 20 miles (32 km) from Nam to detonate *Bravo.* An engineer punched the button on the control panel to start the automatic timer. Needles twitched inside glass gauges. Engines hummed. Equipment beeped. Lights flashed from red to yellow to green, counting down the minutes to *Bravo*'s detonation.

Scientists and other officials at bunkers such as this one in Bikini Atoll directed the detonation of nuclear devices as well as managed the instrumentation that recorded the detonations and their effects.

TRAPPED BY RADIOACTIVE FALLOUT

Dr. John Clark commanded the nine scientists in the bunker near the *Bravo* detonation site. The scientists were in radio contact with their superiors on board the command ship, the USS *Curtiss*. Helicopters would pick them up after the test.

Within seconds of detonation, the men said it felt as if an earthquake had rocked the bunker. Concrete walls creaked. Seawater gushed into the bunker through a broken pipe. Fourteen minutes later, the men placed a Geiger counter outside. The radiation count climbed rapidly, signaling that radioactive fallout had reached the bunker. The helicopter pickup had to be canceled. It was too dangerous to send the choppers in. The men in the bunker would have to hunker down and wait.

Only one room in the bunker was not radioactive. The men locked themselves inside that room and turned off the air-conditioning to prevent it from pulling radioactive air into the bunker. The bunker's gasoline-powered generator failed, plunging the men into darkness. They also lost radio contact with the *Curtiss*, which had moved farther away to avoid radiation contamination.

"We were not exactly a happy bunch as we sat around in that small black room," Clark said during a later interview. "The entire building soon got hot and sticky. Only a few yards away in the construction camp were steaks we had planned on having for breakfast. Instead we were munching C-rations [canned food distributed by the military when fresh food is unavailable]." Twelve hours later, *Curtiss* moved close enough for radio contact. Officials sent three choppers to rescue the men. Clark and his team draped themselves in bedsheets with holes cut out for their eyes. Like Halloween ghosts, they dashed from the bunker to their jeeps and sped to the landing pad where helicopters whisked them away to the *Curtiss*.

SUNRISE IN THE WEST

Meanwhile, morning dawned on Rongelap Atoll, about 100 miles (161 km) from the blast site. Children fed chickens and played with their dogs. Women split coconuts for breakfast. Men made coffee and readied their canoes so they could go fishing later.

At 6:45 a.m., *Bravo* exploded with one thousand times the force of the bomb that the United States had dropped on Hiroshima in 1945. In fact, *Bravo* was the most powerful nuclear device the United States would ever detonate. It created a fireball nearly 4 miles (6 km) wide, vaporizing part of Nam. It left a crater in the ocean floor 1 mile (1.6 km) wide. *Bravo*'s mushroom cloud soared nearly 25 miles (40 km) high.

The dark areas in this aerial photo from 2011 show the crater created by the 1954 detonation of the *Bravo* H-bomb. Coral reefs in the area are still deeply gouged.

Rongelap mayor John Anjain later described what happened in his village. "I saw what appeared to be the sunrise but it was in the west. It was truly beautiful with many colors. Then something like smoke filled the entire sky, and shortly after that a strong and warm wind—as in a typhoon—swept across Rongelap. All the people heard the great sound of the explosion."

Everything on Rongelap returned to normal in a few minutes. The islanders continued with their morning activities. "Once the sound of the explosion died out everyone began cooking," Anjain said. "Some made donuts and others cooked rice. Some men went fishing, including myself."

WHAT WENT WRONG?

US military officials defended their decision not to remove the Rongelapese. Major general Percy Clarkson, the commander of Operation Castle, said, "The natives were not evacuated prior to the detonation because, on the basis of information available to us, it was not considered necessary and no fallout was expected in the inhabited areas." However, the people on Rongelap received as much radiation as did the Japanese who were only 2 miles (3 km) from ground zero in the nuclear bombings of World War II. The chairman of the Atomic Energy Commission (AEC)—a US agency established after the war to regulate peacetime atomic technology—was determined to keep the event secret. But a newspaper in Cincinnati, Ohio, learned what had happened and broke the story on March 11, 1954.

Under pressure to respond, the AEC issued a press release, stating that "during the course of routine atomic tests in the Marshall Islands, twenty-eight United States personnel [American weathermen on Rongerik] and two hundred thirty-six residents were transported from neighboring atolls to Kwajalein as a precautionary measure. These individuals were unexpectedly exposed to some radioactivity. There were no burns. All were reported well. After the completion of the atomic tests, the natives will be returned to their homes."

As news of the event reached the world, the American public reacted in horror. The White House received more than one hundred letters and telegrams each day calling for a halt to atmospheric nuclear testing. In November 1958, President Eisenhower declared a temporary halt to additional atmospheric testing. Such tests later resumed and continued until 1963.

But it was not until 1982 that the US government officially corrected its misstatements about Rongelap. The Department of Defense admitted that the event had been "the worst single incident of fallout exposures in the US atmospheric testing program." The Department of Defense went on to clarify that the people on Rongelap had, in fact, suffered acute radiation poisoning.

ACCIDENT OR COVER-UP?

Why did the US government choose not to evacuate the people of Rongelap? The US military knew that *Bravo* was a bigger and more powerful nuclear weapon than any that had come before. And weather reports suggested the winds would carry radioactive fallout to the island. Yet officials went ahead with the test and then covered up the truth about the impact of radiation poisoning on humans. Some historians believe US officials weren't fully aware of the risks they were taking and did not choose to intentionally cause harm.

But Holly M. Barker, an author and anthropology professor at the University of Washington who has studied the Rongelap issues, disagrees. She says, "I don't think the incidents surrounding *Bravo* were a mistake. For smaller tests before *Bravo,* the United States relocated downwind populations. For the *Bravo* event, the largest test ever conducted by the United States, the government purposefully decided not to remove the people before the detonation. Even knowing the winds were blowing from ground zero to the inhabited atolls on the morning of the test, officials decided to detonate *Bravo.*"

As news of the US nuclear testing in the Marshall Islands spread around the globe, protesters expressed their outrage—and fears. The United States, however, was not alone in developing nuclear weaponry at the time. The United Kingdom, for example, had an H-bomb program too—also tested in the Pacific Ocean--against which protesters in London *(above)* marched in creative style in 1957.

Barker continues, "A naval ship anchored off Rongelap when *Bravo* exploded recorded the high level of radiation arriving at the island. The ship left without taking the Rongelapese, knowing they were staying in a contaminated environment. Two days later, the US government returned and placed the people in a top secret medical program to study the effects of radiation on human beings. *Bravo* was not an accident. There are investigations after accidents, but there were no inquiries after the *Bravo* event to discover how and why the people were exposed to radiation."

Rokko Langinbelik *(above)* was a young girl when she was exposed to radiation on her home island of Rongelap after the United States detonated *Bravo* over Bikini Atoll. In the years since then, the US Department of Energy (DOE) has met regularly with islanders to monitor health concerns and other issues related to the bombings. In this photo from a 2005 meeting with the DOE in Majuro Atoll, Langinbelik holds a sign expressing her views of the nuclear test program.

CHAPTER FIVE

RONGELAP'S RADIATION REFUGEES

From the beginning of the testing program the United States has treated us like animals in a scientific experiment for their studies. They think of us as guinea pigs.

—JOHN ANJAIN, MAYOR OF RONGELAP, 1981

On March 3, 1954, two days after the *Bravo* explosion, a navy ship and a seaplane returned to Rongelap. Two men, Oscar DeBrum (who later became an official of the Marshall Islands) and Governor Wiles of Kwajalein got off the plane and climbed into a small naval boat. "As the boat reached the shore, Mr. Oscar cried out to the people to get on board and forget about personal belongings, for whoever thought of staying behind could die," Mayor Anjain recalled when writing about that day in 1968. Other boats from the ship landed on the beach to evacuate the people. "None of the people went back to their houses, but immediately got on the boats to board the ship that would take them away. Those who were sick and old were evacuated by plane. We were allowed to bring only what we were wearing—nothing else."

Rokko Langinbelik was twelve years old when *Bravo* exploded. She remembered the day the Americans finally evacuated Rongelap. "A boat arrived and they told us we all had to go on it. I was scared and confused. None of us wanted to go. As we loaded the ship they washed us down with water," she said during a newspaper interview many years later. She continued, "They used this small machine [Geiger counter] that they ran over our bodies and after they would give us soap to wash again. Then they would check us again. I went through this routine about three times before they would let me go. We were like animals; it was no different from herding pigs into a gate."

Lijon Eknilang, too, was a child when *Bravo* exploded. On that day, she was with her family on a tiny island near Rongelap, fishing and collecting coconuts. After the US naval ship evacuated Rongelap, it moved to Lijon's island to pick up the people there. "The American personnel on the ship told the people to take all their clothes off," Lijon said. "Men and women—fathers and daughters, mothers and sons, and relatives that it was extremely taboo to disrobe in front of—were forced to stand naked together while the ship's personnel hosed the people down with water."

UNDER A MICROSCOPE

The Americans took the islanders to the US military base at Kwajalein for medical care. Nearly all the Rongelapese showed signs of radiation poisoning. "We were very sick and in much pain, with body burns and bleeding on our necks and feet," Anjain recalled in 1981. The islanders also suffered from loss of appetite along with nausea and diarrhea. Their hair fell out. Painful, bloody sores covered their bodies.

The Rongelap people lived with terrible fear. They thought radiation was contagious, like a virus or bacteria. Isao Eknilang, one of Lijon's relatives, said, "We were very isolated on Kwajalein. Our relatives were afraid to visit for fear they would get radiation from us."

American medical staff on Kwajalein studied the Rongelap islanders for three months. Rokko described the routine: "We were put in military barracks. During the day they would take us to the lagoon to swim. We had to soak in the lagoon from about 9:00 a.m. to around 11:00 a.m. We would wash with special soap and then

THE NOT-SO-LUCKY DRAGON

The Rongelap people were not the only ones affected by *Bravo*'s fallout. The Japanese fishing vessel *Lucky Dragon* 5 *(below)* was cruising about 75 miles (120 km) from Bikini when *Bravo* exploded. Radioactive ash fell over the boat for three hours. The fishermen called it death ash. When the *Lucky Dragon* reached Japan two weeks later, the crew members were suffering acute radiation sickness. They had headaches, bleeding gums, blisters, and their hair fell out.

The ship's radio operator, Aikichi Kuboyama, died seven months later from sickness caused by the radiation. Before his death, he said, "I pray I am the last victim of an atomic or hydrogen bomb." Other crew members died of probable radiation-related illnesses over the next few years.

The event caused an international outcry. Japan, more than any nation on Earth, had suffered a horrific toll from the aftereffects of the atomic bombs dropped over two of its cities in 1945. By August 1955, thirty-two million Japanese people, an estimated 36 percent of the entire population at the time, signed a petition calling for a ban on nuclear testing. The last US atmospheric nuclear test took place in Nevada in 1963, although underground nuclear testing continued until 1992. The *Lucky Dragon* is on display in a Tokyo exhibition hall.

The *Lucky Dragon* incident inspired the 1954 sci-fi horror movie *Godzilla*. This story of a mutant, fire-breathing sea monster that attacks Japan was spawned by the era's nuclear testing programs.

The *Lucky Dragon 5*, on display in a Tokyo exhibition hall, is a reminder to all of the horrors of radiation and atomic bomb testing.

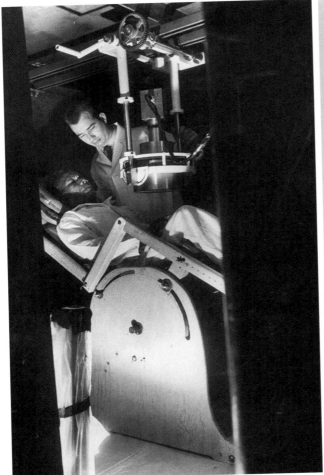

In 1957 an islander from Rongelap undergoes testing with a gamma ray spectrometer to measure the amount of radiation in his body from the *Bravo* explosion. Participation in medical monitoring such as this is ongoing among the impacted populations of the Marshall Islands.

they would check us again with the small machine. They would extract blood almost every day from the tips of my fingers. They also cut samples of our skin. They cut samples from my neck, foot and arms. Never once did they explain why they were doing these things."

Blood tests showed very low white blood cell counts, proof the radiation had damaged the islanders' bone marrow. Scientists later estimated the islanders received 175 roentgens in just a few hours. Most people are exposed to less than 20 roentgens in a lifetime.

TO EJIT—AND BACK TO RONGELAP

Because Rongelap remained too dangerous for human habitation, the AEC resettled the Rongelap islanders on Ejit. This small, uninhabited island in the Majuro Atoll is nearly 300 miles (483 km) from Kwajalein. The Rongelap people lived on Ejit for three years. During this time, vines and weeds overtook their village in Rongelap. Thatched-roof huts sagged, letting in rain that ruined everything left behind in the rushed evacuation. The church burned down after a lightning strike.

By 1957 ten international scientific organizations had conducted radiological surveys of Rongelap. The AEC reported Rongelap was again safe for human habitation, even though the commission knew that "the levels of [radio]activity are higher than those found in other inhabited locations in the world." Even so, the AEC felt there would be scientific value in allowing the Rongelapese to return home. So US construction crews built a new village on Rongelap, complete with homes, a church, a meetinghouse, a clinic, and a school. In July 1957, a small US naval ship carried the islanders and their belongings and animals—sixty chickens, forty pigs, six dogs, one cat, and a duck—from Ejit back to Rongelap. The US government provided a year's worth of canned food, warning the islanders not to eat anything growing on the island, including coconuts and crabs. Dr. Robert Conard, an American physician partially responsible for the decision to allow the Rongelapese to return home, wrote in a confidential memo in 1957 that "the various [radioactive materials] present [on Rongelap] can be traced from the soil, through the food chain, and into human beings."

On arrival, the islanders gathered together on the ship to pray and sing hymns before disembarking. As they got off the ship, they saw a sign the Americans had placed on the beach: "Greetings, Rongelap People. We hope your return to your atoll is a thing of joy and your hearts are happy."

ONGOING MONITORING

After the islanders' return, US medical teams routinely visited Rongelap to examine the people. The most common medical problem the teams observed was thyroid disease, a condition linked to radiation exposure. (Radiation concentrates in the thyroid gland, which produces several important hormones necessary for survival.) At least one-third of the people exposed to radiation developed thyroid tumors. Some were cancerous. In those cases, medical staff transported patients to US hospitals on the mainland where surgeons removed the cancerous thyroid glands, necessitating the lifelong use of thyroid medication.

Blood counts never returned to normal in some people. John Anjain's son, Lekoj, later died of leukemia (a cancer of the bone marrow in which the marrow can no longer produce enough healthy blood cells), another disease related to radiation exposure.

JOHN ANJAIN

Born in 1921, John Anjain was mayor of Rongelap Atoll on March 1, 1954, when the US military detonated *Bravo*. Anjain and four family members eventually required surgery to remove radiation-related thyroid tumors. Anjain's infant son Lekoj was exposed to the heavy radioactive fallout that drifted to Rongelap. Lekoj died in 1972 from leukemia at the age of nineteen.

John Anjain spent fifty years of his life writing and talking about what happened in Rongelap. He testified before committees in New York; Washington, DC; and Japan. He warned the world about the dangers of radiation. He pursued fair treatment for Marshall islanders affected by nuclear testing and radioactive fallout. He forced the US government to undertake independent studies of radiation levels at Rongelap, resulting in agreements to financially compensate each person affected by the *Bravo* incident.

Anjain died at a hospital in Honolulu, Hawaii, in 2004 at the age of eighty-three from stomach cancer. He was buried on Mejatto Island in the Kwajalein Atoll.

Several children showed signs of retarded physical growth and were significantly shorter than Marshallese children who had not been exposed to radiation.

Women exposed to radiation suffered miscarriages and stillbirths. Some delivered babies with birth defects. The Rongelap language had no words for these defects, so the islanders devised new terms: sailfish baby (a child born with spina bifida, an exposed spine), coconut head baby (a baby born with hydrocephalus, an abnormal collection of fluid in the brain), and jellyfish babies (babies born without or with missing bones).

Ongoing monitoring found the level of several radioactive materials in the islanders' bodies had risen by twenty to sixty times in one year. Plants and animals remained radioactive. Yet scientists and the US government insisted it was safe to live on Rongelap. Mistrustful of the reports, John Anjain pleaded with the United States to relocate his people but was repeatedly refused. He condemned the United States for its failure to help.

GREENPEACE TO THE RESCUE

The islanders became convinced they must leave Rongelap for the future of their children. Rongelap leaders eventually appealed to Greenpeace, an international environmental organization. In May 1985, the Greenpeace ship *Rainbow Warrior* moved more than three hundred people—the entire population—from Rongelap to Mejatto, a small island in the Kwajalein Atoll. International journalists went along to chronicle the voyage. Only pigs and chickens remained on Rongelap because the people feared the animals might carry radiation to Mejatto.

Neither the US nor Marshallese governments knew about the move to Mejatto until after it occurred. Critics of the move claimed Greenpeace and other outside groups had influenced the islanders to leave Rongelap unnecessarily. Rongelap senator Jeton Anjain denied those allegations. "[The move] was instigated by me and my people as a result of the American nuclear testing program.

Rongelap islanders—convinced of the dangers of remaining on Rongelap—evacuated the island in 1985 on board the *Rainbow Warrior*. The Greenpeace ship took them to an island in Kwajalein Atoll.

We don't need brilliant scientists to come and tell us we're not sick. We have had health problems on Rongelap from the beginning—we are having them today and we will have them for the indefinite future."

Since the *Bravo* bomb test of 1954, Rongelap's radiation refugees have moved or been evacuated from Rongelap to Kwajalein; to Ejit; back to Rongelap; and to Mejatto in the Kwajalein Atoll. Many eventually made their way to the United States, making new homes in California, Oregon, Washington, Hawaii, and in other states. Others ended up in various parts of the Marshall Islands.

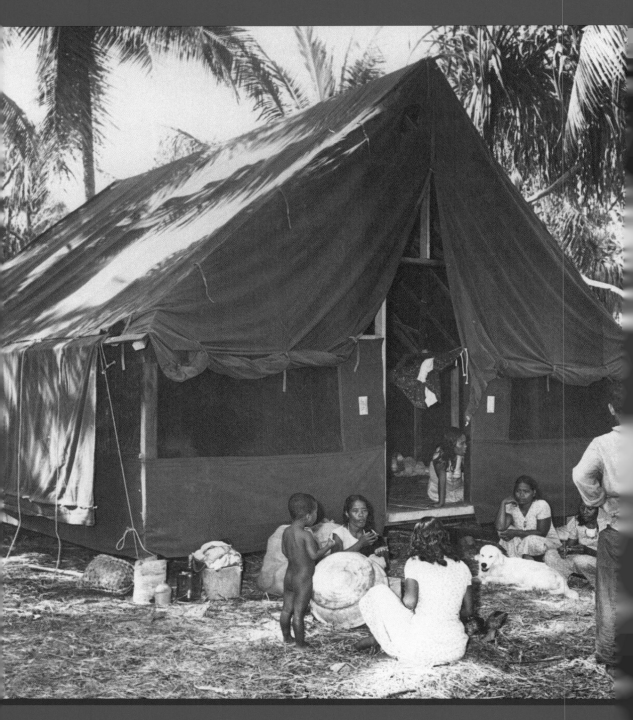

Bikini islanders sit outside an army tent on Rongerik Atoll after the US Navy moved them there in 1946.

CHAPTER SIX

BIKINI'S **NUCLEAR** NOMADS

The Americans told us they did not know how much the bomb would hurt Bikini. They told us after they tested the bomb and Bikini is good again, they will bring us back. The American is a liar-man. His promise is not kept.

—ANDREW JAKEO, 1978

Unlike the people of Rongelap, the Bikinians were not doused in radioactive fallout. Instead, the US Navy moved them from their ancestral home on Bikini to the uninhabited Rongerik Atoll in March 1946. Four months later, the navy detonated the first two bombs of Operation Crossroads.

US Navy commodore Ben Wyatt, who had helped convince the Bikinians to move to Rongerik, told reporters that Rongerik was a bigger island than Bikini with richer natural resources. In reality, it was one-fourth the size of Bikini and food was scarce. The island's coconuts were smaller, and some of the fish in the lagoon were poisonous.

STARVING ON RONGERIK

The Americans left the Bikinians with fresh water and a month's supply of food. But one month's supply of food wasn't enough. Over the following months, the Bikinians suffered severe food shortages and hunger. A fire destroyed many of the coconut trees on Rongerik

The US Navy and Marshall islanders constructed new homes on Rongerik for the Bikini refugees who were relocated there after the test bomb explosions of 1946. Thus began decades of resettlement for the exiles, whose home island remains unsafe for human habitation.

the next spring, worsening the food situation. As a result, Bikinians took some children and elders to live with relatives on Rongelap, a few hours away by sailing craft, and to ask for food supplies to take back to Bikini.

The international press had publicized the poor treatment of the Bikinians. Concerned about negative reaction to the news, the US Navy wanted to move the Bikinians to a safer location at Ujelang Atoll. But the navy hadn't realized that the AEC was relocating the people of Enewetak Atoll to Ujelang in preparation for nuclear testing on Enewetak. Like losers in a game of musical chairs, the Bikinians were returned to Rongerik by the navy.

By the end of 1947, the Bikinians on Rongerik were starving. They had a diet of only thin gruel made of flour and water, fish that were mildly poisonous, and the edible part of trees and shrubbery. Marshallese politician Charles Domnick recalled what he saw as a child when a ship he was on stopped at Rongerik that year. "I had my first dramatic, horrid, eye-opening and shocking sight of emaciated people—people who were just skin and bones. They were left in Rongerik to fend for their own survival. The image I saw is not dissimilar from that of the emaciated Jews when they were freed from Nazi concentration camps after World War II."

BIKINI'S NUCLEAR NOMADS

"The people deserve a lot more than they have been given by the richest country in the world," a *New York Times* editorial said about the situation on October 3, 1947. As a result of public pressure, the United States temporarily relocated the Bikinians from Rongerik to Kwajalein in March 1948. There, they lived in tents erected beside a busy concrete airstrip. "We lived a strange life on Kwajalein," said Kilon Bauno, a Bikini elder. "We were frightened by all the airplanes that continuously landed very close to our homes. We were also frustrated by the small amount of space in which we were permitted to move around. We had to depend on the US military for everything."

Six months later, the United States moved the Bikinians yet again, this time to the uninhabited, Hobbit-sized island of Kili 500 miles (805 km) from Bikini. The tiny island has no harbor or lagoon. It is isolated, and because of rough waters, it cannot be reached by sea several months out of the year. In fact, the US military often dropped emergency rations by air.

But Kili was not the last stop for Bikini's nuclear nomads. Nearly twenty years later, in 1969, the United States began a decontamination project on Bikini. Workers bulldozed vegetation, replaced some of the soil in planned living areas, and added potassium fertilizer to reduce the amount of radiation that plants would absorb from the remaining soil. They also constructed new housing and community buildings. AEC officials then announced that "there's virtually no radiation left [on Bikini] and we can find no discernible effect on either plant or animal life."

Some Bikinians were ecstatic. "Once I heard the US government was proclaiming that Bikini was safe and free from poison [the Marshallese had no word for radiation], I began to have overwhelming thoughts of joy," Bikinian Pero Joel said.

Between 1969 and 1971, several families (eventually about 140 people) moved from Kili back to Bikini. "I worked on Bikini planting crops, pulling weeds, refurbishing the island. I was so happy. We belonged on Bikini because it is the place that God had given us," Joel said.

Other families, however, worried about radiation levels on Bikini and chose to remain on Kili. As it turned out, their fears were justified. Further monitoring on Bikini revealed radiation in well water and in locally grown coconuts and breadfruit. Additionally,

For a short period in the late 1960s and the early 1970s, islanders were allowed to return to Bikini (left). The US government eventually confirmed the fears of radiation contamination expressed by most Bikinians, resettling—yet again—those who had chosen to move back.

THE BIKINI NATIONAL ANTHEM

Bikini poet and singer Lore Kessibuki wrote this song as he watched Bikini slip from sight when the Americans moved his people to Rongerik in 1946.

No longer can I stay; it's true.

No longer can I live in peace and harmony.

No longer can I rest on my sleeping mat and pillow

Because of my island and the life I once knew there.

The thought is overwhelming

Rendering me helpless and in great despair.

My spirit leaves, drifting around and far away

Where it becomes caught in a current of immense power—

And only then do I find tranquility.

the amount of radiation Bikinians were actually ingesting was nearly one hundred times higher than originally calculated. "We just plain goofed," Gordon Dunning of the AEC said at a later government hearing about the botched Bikini resettlement.

"It became evident that [radioactive] intake in the plant food chain had been significantly miscalculated in terms of human consumption," James A. Joseph of the Interior Department told Congress in 1978 when requesting $15 million to move the Bikinians off Bikini.

In a 1989 interview, Pero Joel remembered that once again, the United States told the Bikinians to pack up and leave their homeland. "The Americans and their scientists came back saying that we had to leave Bikini. They said we had ingested too much poison and it wasn't safe to live on Bikini anymore. The Americans first told us that it was safe to live here. Now they are telling us to leave. We were so heartbroken we didn't know what to do." In the end, some of the Bikini islanders returned to Kili or to other islands in the area. Still others resettled in the United States. Pero Joel died of cancer in 2002 and is buried on Ejit Island.

In this photo from 2008, Bikinians on Kili greet Kessai Note *(center)*, president of the Marshall Islands, and US ambassador Greta Morris *(directly behind him)*. The officials were there to mark the sixtieth anniversary of the 1948 Kili relocation.

CHAPTER SEVEN

A BRIGHTER FUTURE?

The total yield of the tests in the Marshall Islands was equivalent to 7,200 Hiroshima bombs. That works out to an average of more than 1.6 Hiroshima bombs per day for the 12-year nuclear testing program in the Marshalls.

—JONATHAN M. WEISGALL, ATTORNEY AND AUTHOR, SPEAKING TO THE US CONGRESS IN 2003 ON BEHALF OF THE MARSHALL ISLANDERS

Islands blasted into oblivion. Hundreds of people shunted around the Marshall Islands for decades. Radioactive contamination of homes. Horrific physical suffering, cancers, and premature deaths. What, if anything, did the United States learn from the nuclear testing in the Marshall Islands?

On the practical side, scientists learned how to successfully build and detonate a variety of nuclear devices. *Bravo*'s radioactive fallout forced the world to reassess the dangers of atmospheric nuclear testing and to eventually halt such testing. And whether by accident or intention, the fallout on Rongelap allowed scientists and doctors to study how radiation affects humans over time.

However, the people of Bikini and Rongelap Atolls paid an enormous price for this new knowledge. According to the Embassy of the Republic of the Marshall Islands website, one study of the Marshall Islands showed that almost half the nation was dusted by radioactive fallout from the US nuclear weapons tests. According to the embassy, "The Marshallese people still confront medical problems, environmental contamination, displacement and social upheaval resulting from the testing program."

The Bikinians and the Rongelapese endured a range of medical problems as a result of the nuclear tests. These included radiation burns; thyroid tumors, some of which were cancerous; other forms of cancer such as leukemia and cancer of the gastrointestinal tract; miscarriages; and deformed infants. The Bikinians and the Rongelapese, once self-sustaining communities, became a dependent people, relying—out of necessity—on the United States for food and provisions. Forced evacuations tore apart close-knit communities.

Aside from the hardships of being forced into a nomadic existence, the Marshallese felt an acute loss of status. Ownership of even small parcels of land—passed lovingly from mother to daughter for generations—was an important part of the society's culture. Bikinian Jukwa Jakeo said during a 1987 interview, "To all Marshallese, land is gold. If you were an owner of land, you would be held up as a very important figure in our society. Without land you would be viewed as a person of no consequence. But land on Bikini is now poison land."

SEEKING COMPENSATION FOR BIKINI

After the United States won control of the Marshall Islands from Japan during World War II, the islands were administered in turn by the United Nations, the US Navy, and the US Department of the Interior. The islands have been an independent republic only since 1982. The United States and the people of Bikini have entered into a number of agreements over the years in recognition of the contributions and sacrifices resulting from the US nuclear testing program. For example, the 1983 Compact of Free Association (an agreement between the United States and the Marshall Islands) provided $150 million in compensation payments to people of the Bikini, Enewetak, Rongelap, and Utrik Atolls.

In 1988 the government of the Marshall Islands established the Marshall Islands Nuclear Claims Tribunal in accordance with a previous agreement with the United States. The tribunal's purpose is to study damages and to make additional awards to affected Marshall islanders. In 1991 the tribunal implemented a compensation program for a list of thirty-six medical conditions deemed to have resulted from radiation exposure during the nuclear testing program. By the end of 2003, the tribunal had paid more than $83 million for such injuries.

In 2001, after years of deliberation, the Nuclear Claims Tribunal awarded more than $563 million to the people of Bikini. The money is for the past and future loss (until 2027) of the lands of Bikini Atoll, for the hardships suffered by the Bikinians as a result

John Anjain *(left)* with his niece, Senator Abacca Anjain-Maddison, as she reads a translation of his statement about the exposure to *Bravo* nuclear fallout to the Nuclear Claims Tribunal in Majuro in November 2001. The struggle for recognition of suffering related to the US nuclear test programs in the Marshall Islands—and for fair and just compensation—is ongoing.

PAYMENT PAST DUE!

For decades, the people of the Marshall Islands have sought full and just compensation for the harm and suffering they experienced as a result of the US nuclear testing program. Among other efforts, the government of the Marshall Islands has worked through the US court system. The process has been complex and convoluted. Through the years, the United States has paid relatively small amounts of money to displaced islanders and to those contaminated by radioactive fallout. For example, in 1956, the United States gave $25,000 to each Bikinian living on Kili.

In 1986 the US Congress approved the 1983 Compact of Free Association. It included a provision that prohibits Marshall islanders from filing future legal cases in US courts. It also dismissed all court cases in exchange for a $150 million compensation trust fund. However, that money was insufficient to pay for cleanup of contaminated islands and for compensation to affected islanders.

In 2001 the Marshall Islands Nuclear Claims Tribunal awarded $563 million to former residents of Bikini Atoll. The Bikinians have received only $2.3 million of that money. In 2006 Bikinians filed a lawsuit seeking compensation under the Fifth Amendment of the US Constitution for the taking of their property and for the US government's refusal to adequately fund the Nuclear Claims

In a US congressional hearing in 1985, Lieutenant General John L. Pickitt *(in uniform, at microphone)*, director of the Defense Nuclear Agency, testifies that fallout from Operation Crossroads did not expose soldiers to dangerous amounts of radiation. Along with impacted Marshall islanders, US veterans of the nuclear test program continue to struggle for recognition of and compensation for their suffering.

Tribunal award. In 2009 a US appeals court ruled that those claims were settled in 1986 and that the islanders had no right to additional funds. Attorneys for the Bikinians then took the case to the US Supreme Court. However, justices dismissed the case without comment in 2010.

of their relocations, and for the restoration of Bikini to a safe and productive status. However, the tribunal halted payments in 2007 for lack of money, and the compensation trust fund provided by the United States is also nearly out of money.

American author and filmmaker Jack Niedenthal is the trust liaison for the people of Bikini Atoll. The Bikinians employ him to manage the funds allocated by the United States to the Bikinians. He also functions as liaison to the media, agencies of the US government, scientists, and others who work on Bikini or have business dealings with it. He says, "The Bikinians' attempt to collect the $563 million settlement awarded by the Nuclear Claims Tribunal was thrown out of the US Supreme Court in 2010." (The tribunal had sought full compensation through the US court system, but when the case came before the Supreme Court, the justices declined to hear the case and rejected it without explaining their decision.) "The Bikinians' only avenue for further funding is the U.S. Congress. We continue to lobby Congress but doubt it will help."

From left to right: Bikini trust liaison Jack Niedenthal stands with Marshallese politicians Councilman Wilson Note, Councilman Banjo Joel, Senator Tomaki Juda, and Mayor Alson Kelen, and with Bikini attorney Jonathan Weisgall in front of the US Supreme Court in 2010. The effort to receive just compensation for the Marshallese people impacted by US nuclear test programs has faced many hurdles over the years.

CLEANUP EFFORTS AT BIKINI ATOLL

American scientists have been closely monitoring the animals, plants, and soil of Bikini since 1975. Long-term experiments to decontaminate the island—a process called remediation—have been ongoing since 1969. For example, adding potassium fertilizer to agricultural areas reduces radiation in food grown on the land by 95 percent. Removing the top 10 inches (25 cm) of soil around living areas prior to new construction and replacing it with crushed coral has proven effective on Rongelap and will be used on Bikini as well. In 1985 Eneu, one of the Bikini Atoll islands, was declared safe for habitation. It will be the main base of operations for the cleanup of the other islands of Bikini Atoll.

Dr. Terry Hamilton works for Lawrence Livermore National Laboratory in Livermore, California. One of the lab's missions is the cleanup of Rongelap. Hamilton is a physicist and expert on radiology in the environment. During a 2010 magazine interview, he

Monitoring radiation levels in radiation-exposed areas of the Marshall Islands is an ongoing effort. For example, Lawrence Livermore National Laboratory and the Rongelap government run a garden project on Rongelap to study twenty-first-century radiation levels in food plants grown locally. This effort is one of many ways to track the degree to which local soils have been decontaminated.

said about Bikini, "People could possibly resettle on Bikini based on the data we're getting from the remediation and resettlement effort at Rongelap. If this remediation strategy is pursued, we estimate the natural background dose [of radiation] combined with the nuclear-test-related dose on the islands of Bikini and Rongelap would be less than the typical background dose in the United States." When can people safely return to Bikini? Five Years? Ten? Twenty? No one can say for sure, but Hamilton hopes "that we see full resettlement of the affected atolls in my lifetime."

COMPENSATION AND CLEANUP AT RONGELAP

As with Bikini, Rongelap has been engaged for many years in lawsuits and hearings attempting to obtain compensation for the damages done by nuclear testing. The people have received money from the Nuclear Claims Tribunal settlements of 1983 and 1991. In addition, after fifteen years of legal action, the tribunal ruled in 2007 that the United States owed Rongelap islanders $1 billion in damages for radiation illnesses, the contamination of their atoll, emotional distress, and the past and present loss of lands.

WORLD HERITAGE SITE

The United Nations Educational, Scientific and Cultural Organization (UNESCO) has identified hundreds of cultural and natural sites around the world that offer universal value to global citizens. In August 2010, the organization's World Heritage Committee added the Bikini Atoll Nuclear Test Site to its World Heritage List. Bikini Atoll was recognized for the role the nuclear bomb tests played in shaping global culture in the second half of the twentieth century.

In the words of UNESCO itself, "The violence exerted on the natural, geophysical and living elements by nuclear weapons illustrates the relationship which can develop between man and the environment. This is reflected in the ecosystems and the terrestrial, marine and underwater landscapes of Bikini Atoll. The nuclear tests changed the history of Bikini Atoll and the Marshall Islands, through the displacement of inhabitants and the human irradiation and contamination caused by [radioactivity] produced by the tests."

A key part of that decision reflected the harm and suffering that resulted from the premature return of the Rongelap people to their contaminated atoll in 1957. The award is the largest made by the tribunal, but little of that money has reached the Rongelap people because the United States has not adequately funded the tribunal. Rongelap mayor James Matayoshi said the islanders would file suit in US courts to enforce the tribunal's award.

As of 2013, the United States has made progress in reducing radioactivity on Rongelap by removing layers of contaminated soil and replacing it with clean crushed coral and spreading potassium fertilizer over crop areas. Scientific studies suggest that radiation exposure there is similar to the natural background radiation elsewhere on Earth, and the US government has declared Rongelap safe for human habitation. Seventy construction workers and their families live on the island, and nearly fifty new houses await occupation.

However, not everyone agrees that Rongelap is safe for humans. In August 2012, Jelton Anjain (Jeton's son and John's nephew) spoke at an antinuclear conference in Hiroshima, Japan. "Despite the fact the islands are not ready and [are] still contaminated, the U.S. Congress is urging our people to move back," he said. "Our people are still uneasy about going back as we know the islands are still not clean. People do not trust the Department of Energy. They are not truthful about the cleanup and safety of the islands."

Anjain does not speak for all the Rongelapese, however. In 2012 Matayoshi told reporters, "People are in high spirits about the possibility of resettling. The house construction is on track." Mayor Matayoshi believes successful resettlement will depend on additional housing and a new school and clinic. He also says the people must have further reassurances about safe levels of radiation exposure and cleanup of other islands in the atoll. Cleanup work has focused on Rongelap's main island and not on the other sixty islands of the atoll, where people traditionally fish and gather food. Matayoshi also wants to see ongoing funding for resettlement and radiation protection work.

When can Rongelap's radiation refugees return home? Five years? Ten? It's likely they can return one day, but no one can be certain when. "It's up to the Rongelapese to determine the best path for the future," professor Barker at the University of Washington, says. "The community lives with the consequences so they should determine what is best for them. If it were me and my family, I couldn't imagine living there."

Rongelap mayor James Matayoshi, in a photo from 2012, expresses guarded optimism about the potential for resettlement of the island. He recognizes a need for additional cleanup and other safety measures to protect the Rongelapese if they return to their home.

COUNTING UP

In 1946 the US military began a countdown for the first nuclear test bombing in the Marshall Islands. Since then, another type of count is under way—a counting up of decades, marking out the time until the displaced people of Bikini and Rongelap Atolls can safely return to their ancestral homeland.

Many people echo the thoughts of Jack Niedenthal. He sums up the nuclear testing program by observing that "the nuclear testing on Bikini Atoll was a reality check for the rest of the world. Lore Kessibuki, a Bikinian leader who died in 1994, once said he felt proud the people of Bikini sacrificed not only their land, but in some cases their lives, so that mankind will never have to experience an all-out nuclear war. The devastating impact on the lives of the people of Bikini must never be forgotten; the careless testing of the nuclear bombs on Bikini was a mistake that should never be repeated."

SOURCE NOTES

5   Bob Hope, *So This Is Peace* (New York: Simon & Schuster, 1947), 1.

5   John Anjain, quoted in Barbara Rose Johnston and Holly M. Barker, *Consequential Damages of Nuclear War: The Rongelap Report* (Walnut Creek, CA: Left Coast Press, 2008), 11–12.

5–6   Ibid., 12.

7   Harold Wood, quoted in *Radio Bikini*, directed by Robert Stone (New York: IFC Films, 1987), DVD.

9   Ben Wyatt, quoted in Jonathan M. Weisgall, *Operation Crossroads: The Atomic Tests at Bikini Atoll* (Annapolis, MD: Naval Institute Press, 1994), 107.

11   Biamon Lewis, quoted in Jack Niedenthal, *For the Good of Mankind: A History of the People of Bikini and Their Islands*, 2nd ed. (Majuro, Marshall Islands: Bravo Publishers, 2001), 4.

12   William Blandy, quoted in Joint Task Force One Office of the Historian, *Operation Crossroads: The Official Pictorial Record* (New York: Wm. H. Wise & Co., 1946), 6.

12   William Blandy, quoted in *Trinity and Beyond: The Atomic Bomb Movie*, directed by Peter Kuran (Los Angeles: Visual Concept Entertainment, 1995), DVD.

12   Harry Truman, quoted in Weisgall, *Operation Crossroads*, 6.

13   William Blandy, quoted in Weisgall, *Operation Crossroads*, 7.

13   Ibid., 32.

14   Unnamed naval source, quoted in Weisgall, *Operation Crossroads*, 107.

15   Juda Kessibuki, quoted in Jane Dibblin, *Day of Two Suns: US Nuclear Testing and the Pacific Islanders* (London: Virago, 1988), 11.

15   Emso Leviticus, quoted in Niedenthal, *For the Good of Mankind*, 63.

19   William Blandy, quoted in Joint Task Force One, *Operation Crossroads: The Official Pictorial Record*, 6.

22   Bill Chaplin, quoted in Weisgall, *Operation Crossroads*, 182.

22   William Laurence, quoted in Weisgall, *Operation Crossroads*, 184.

22   Harold Wood, quoted in Weisgall, *Operation Crossroads*, 185.

23   William Laurence, quoted in Weisgall, *Operation Crossroads*, 186.

23–24   Gerald Gross, "A-Bomb Sinks 2 Ships and Damages 17: Experiment Success." *Washington Post*, July 1, 1946, http://www.washingtonpost.com/wp-srv/inatl/longterm/flash/july/bikini46.htm.

24 William Blandy, quoted in Gross, "A-Bomb Sinks."

24 William Blandy, quoted in Weisgall, *Operation Crossroads*, 120.

25 Thomas Betts, quoted in Weisgall, *Operation Crossroads*, 158.

26 US Navy press release, quoted in Weisgall, *Operation Crossroads*, 120.

29 William Laurence, quoted in Weisgall, *Operation Crossroads*, 222.

30 Unnamed navy official, quoted in Weisgall, *Operation Crossroads*, 219.

31 Philip Porter, quoted in Weisgall, *Operation Crossroads*, 222.

31 Steven White, quoted in Weisgall, *Operation Crossroads*, 222.

34 John Smitherman, quoted in *Radio Bikini*.

34 Ibid.

39 Weisgall, *Operation Crossroads,* 302.

42 Gene Curbow, quoted in Judith Miller, "4 Veterans Suing U.S. over Exposure in '54 Atom Test," *New York Times*, September 20, 1982.

44 John Clark, quoted in Robert Cahn, "We Were Trapped by Radioactive Fallout," *Saturday Evening Post*, July 20 1957, 17.

46 John Anjain, quoted in Dibblin, *Day of Two Suns*, 25.

46 John Anjain, quoted in Johnston and Barker, *Consequential Damages*, 11.

46 Percy Clarkson, quoted in Robert A. Conard, *Fallout: The Experiences of a Medical Team in the Care of a Marshallese Population Accidently Exposed to Fallout Radiation*, 1992, Medical Department, Brookhaven National Laboratory, accessed August 13, 2013, http://www.osti.gov/bridge/servlets/purl/10117645-4nvHOA/webviewable/10117645.pdf.

46 Atomic Energy Commission press release, quoted in Conard, *Fallout*, 7.

47 US Department of Defense, Defense Nuclear Agency, quoted in Weisgall, *Operation Crossroads*, 304.

47 Holly M. Barker, interviews with the author, February–June 2013.

49 Ibid.

51 John Anjain, quoted in Glenn Alcalay, "Anjain's Life with *Bravo*," *Marshall Islands Journal*, July 30, 2004, http://www.visitrongelap.com/MediaCenter/Press_Releases/pdf/Farewell%20John%20Anjain.pdf.

51 John Anjain, quoted in Johnston and Barker, *Consequential Damages*, 12.

51 Ibid.

51–52 Rokko Langinbelik, quoted in "Remembering the Bomb: A *Marshall Islands Journal* Tribute on the Anniversary of Bikini Day," *Marshall Islands Journal*, February 27, 2004, http://www.visitrongelap.com/MediaCenter/Press_Releases/2004_0227_bravo_50th_anniversary.htm#rokko.

52 Ibid.

52 Lijon Eknilang, quoted in Johnston and Barker, *Consequential Damages*, 101–102.

52 John Anjain, quoted in Alcalay, "Anjain's Life."

52 Isao Eknilang, quoted in Johnston and Barker, *Consequential Damages*, 103.

52, 54 Rokko Langinbelik, quoted in "Remembering the Bomb, *Marshall Islands Journal*."

53 Aikichi Kuboyama, quoted in Mark Schreiber, "Lucky Dragon's Lethal Catch," *Japan Times: Life*, March 18, 2012, http://www.japantimes.co.jp/life/2012/03/18/life/lucky-dragons-lethal-catch/#.UXQ4v0bn-ic.

55 Robert A. Conard, *March 1957 Medical Survey of Rongelap and Utrik People*, Brookhaven National Laboratory, June 1958, https://www.osti.gov/opennet/servlets/purl/16365754-YNQB80/16365754.pdf.

55 Robert Conard, quoted in Thomas Maier, "Cold War Fall Out for Brookhaven National Lab," *Long Island Newsday*, August 21, 2009, http://www.agriculturedefensecoalition.org/sites/default/files/file/nuclear/14J_2009_Nuclear_Testing_Cold_War_Fallout_for_Brookhaven_National_Lab_August_21_2009_Article.pdf.

55 Conard, *Fallout*.

57, 59 Jeton Anjain, quoted in David Robie, *Eyes of Fire: The Last Voyage of the Rainbow Warrior* (Philadelphia: New Society Publishers, 1987), 65.

61 Andrew Jakeo, quoted in Jerry Belcher, "Bikini Island: Lost Again to Radiation," *Los Angeles Times*, July 23, 1978.

63 Charles Domnick, quoted in "Seeking Justice: Remarks by Marshall Islands' Charles Domnick on 58th Anniversary of BRAVO Shot," speaking at Nuclear Survivors Remembrance Day, International Convention Center, Majuro, Republic of the Marshall Islands, *YokweOnline*, March 1, 2012, http://www.yokwe.net/index.php?module=News&func=display&sid=2977.

63 *New York Times* editorial, October 3, 1947, quoted in Weisgall, *Operation Crossroads*, 312.

63 Kilon Bauno, quoted in Niedenthal, *For the Good of Mankind*, 82.

64 Atomic Energy Commission, quoted in *Nuclear Testing in the Marshall Islands: A Chronology of Events*, Marshall Island Embassy, accessed August 13, 2013, http://www.rmiembassyus.org/Nuclear%20Issues.htm#Chronology.

64 Pero Joel, quoted in Niedenthal, *For the Good of Mankind*, 127.

64 Ibid.

65 Gordon Dunning, quoted in Advisory Committee on Human Radiation Experiments, public meeting in Washington, DC, February 15, 1995, http://www.gwu.edu/~nsarchiv/radiation/dir/mstreet/commeet/meet11/trnsc11a.txt.

65 James A. Joseph, quoted in Belcher, "Bikini Island."

65 Pero Joel, quoted in Niedenthal, *For the Good of Mankind*, 127–130.

67 Jonathan M. Weisgall, *Statement of the Peoples of Bikini, Enewetak, Rongelap and Utrik before the House Resources Committee*, July 10, 2003, http://www.bikiniatoll.com/Weisgall%20testimony%207-10-03.pdf.

68 "The US Nuclear Weapons Testing Program," Republic of the Marshall Islands, accessed August 13, 2013, http://www.rmiembassyus.org/Exhib%20Nuclear.htm.

68 Jukwa Jakeo, quoted in Niedenthal, *For the Good of Mankind*, 133.

71 Jack Niedenthal, interviews with author, February–July, 2013.

71 Ibid.

73 Terry Hamilton, quoted in "Return to Rongelap," *Science & Technology Review*, July/August 2010, https://str.llnl.gov/JulAug10/hamilton.html.

73 Ibid.

73 "Bikini Atoll Nuclear Test Site," UNESCO World Heritage Convention, accessed August 13, 2013, http://whc.unesco.org/en/list/1339.

74 Jelton Anjain, quoted in *Moving Back to Rongelap?*, Nuclear Age Peace Foundation, August 20, 2012, http://www.wagingpeace.org/articles/db_article.php?article_id=388.

74 James Matayoshi, quoted in Giff Johnson, "Home at Last," *Marshall Islands Journal*, February 12, 2010, http://www.marshallislandsjournal.com/Journal%20February%2012,%202010.html.

75 Barker, interview with the author.

75 Niedenthal, interview with the author.

Able: the first atomic bomb tested by the US military in the Marshall Islands in 1946 as part of a nuclear testing program called Operation Crossroads. A B-29 bomber dropped the 23,000-ton (23-kiloton) bomb over Bikini Lagoon on July 1 of that year.

atoll: a group of islands surrounding a lagoon, formed as a result of coral growth on a volcano that later sank into the sea

atomic bomb: a nuclear device whose explosion is powered by fission; sometimes referred to as an A-bomb

Atomic Energy Commission (AEC): an agency of the US government formed in 1946 that is responsible for the peacetime development and regulation of atomic energy and nuclear technology

Baker: the second atomic bomb detonated on July 25, 1946, by the United States in the Marshall Islands as part of Operation Crossroads. The bomb exploded underwater in Bikini Lagoon, heavily contaminating the water.

Bravo: the first deliverable hydrogen bomb, detonated in the Bikini Atoll by the United States in 1954. Radioactive fallout covered a vast area, including Rongelap Atoll, whose people bore the brunt of nuclear contamination.

fission: the process of neutrons hitting the nucleus of an atom of a heavy element such as uranium. The neutrons split the uranium into lighter elements. In a fission bomb, the splitting force results in a powerful explosion.

fusion: the process of the nuclei of atoms of lighter-weight elements such as hydrogen combining to form heavier elements. In a fusion bomb, the combining force results in an explosion far more powerful than that of fission bombs.

hydrogen bomb: a nuclear explosion powered by fusion; sometimes referred to as an H-bomb

Manhattan Project: the secret US government research project (1941–1945) that produced the world's first atomic bombs. The work of the Manhattan Project was carried out under the leadership of Colonel Leslie Groves and Dr. J. Robert Oppenheimer at labs across the United States.

Marshall Islands Nuclear Claims Tribunal: Established in 1988, the tribunal was designed to render final judgment on past, present, and future claims made by the government and the people of the Marshall Islands arising from the nuclear testing program. While millions of dollars have been paid, more than $1 billion has been awarded but remains unpaid due to lack of funds.

nuclear bomb: an explosive device that derives its power from nuclear reactions, either fission or fusion or a combination of both. These reactions release huge quantities of energy from small amounts of matter.

Operation Castle: a nuclear testing program conducted by the Atomic Energy Commission and the US Department of Defense to test designs for an aircraft-deliverable nuclear weapon. It consisted of a series of hydrogen bombs detonated at Bikini Atoll. *Bravo*, the first bomb of Operation Castle, sent a cloud of radioactivity over Rongelap Atoll and its people. The other five bombs, all less powerful than *Bravo*, went off as scheduled.

Operation Crossroads: a nuclear testing program conducted by the US military in which the first peacetime atomic bombs—*Able* and *Baker*—were detonated over Bikini Atoll in 1946. The purpose of the project was to investigate how atomic bombs affected naval ships anchored in Bikini's lagoon.

radioactive fallout: residual radioactive material such as dust, ash, or pulverized coral (as at Bikini) propelled into the atmosphere after a nuclear explosion. When the radioactive material settles back to Earth, it is called fallout.

remediation: the removal of a hazardous substance such as radiation or radiation-contaminated materials from the environment

Committee on Radiological Safety in the Marshall Islands. *Radiological Assessments for Resettlement of Rongelap in the Republic of the Marshall Islands.* Washington, DC: National Academies Press, 1994. Accessed June 26, 2013. http://www.nap.edu/openbook.php?record_id=2352&page=R1.

Conard, R. A. *The Experiences of a Medical Team in the Care of a Marshallese Population Accidently Exposed to Fallout Radiation.* 1992. Medical Department, Brookhaven National Laboratory. Accessed June 26, 2013. http://www.osti.gov /bridge/servlets/purl/10117645-4nvHOA/webviewable/10117645.pdf.

Cronkite Eugene P. , Victor P. Bond, Robert A. Conard, N. Raphael Shulman, Richard S. Farr, Stanton H. Cohn, Charles L. Dunham, and L. Eugene Browning. *Response of Human Beings Accidentally Exposed to Significant Fall-out Radiation. Journal of the American Medical Association* 159, no 5 (October 1, 1955): 430–434.

Dibblin, Jane. *Day of Two Suns: US Nuclear Testing and the Pacific Islanders.* London: Virago, 1988.

Ellis, W. S. "A Way of Life Lost: Bikini." *National Geographic* 169 (June 1986): 812–834.

Johnston, Barbara Rose, and Holly M. Barker. *Consequential Damages of Nuclear War: The Rongelap Report.* Walnut Creek, CA: Left Coast Press, 2008.

Lawrence Livermore National Laboratory. "Return to Rongelap." *Science & Technology Review*, July/August 2010. Accessed June 26, 2013. https://str.llnl .gov/JulAug10/hamilton.html.

———. *Rongelap Resettlement Support—Preliminary Report Part 1 In-Situ Gamma Spectrometric Measurements around the Service and Village Area on Rongelap Island.* 2001. Accessed June 26, 2013. http://www.hss.doe.gov/healthsafety/ env_docs/RongelapResettlement.pdf.

Lessard, E. T., R. P. Miltenberger, S. H. Cohn, S. V. Musolino, and R. A. Conard. "Protracted Exposure to Fallout: The Rongelap and Utrik Experience." *Health Physics* 46, no. 3 (March 1984): 511–527.

McHenry, Donald F. *Micronesia, Trust Betrayed: Altruism vs Self Interest in American Foreign Policy.* New York: Carnegie Endowment for International Peace, 1975.

Niedenthal, Jack. *For the Good of Mankind: A History of the People of Bikini and Their Islands.* Majuro, Marshall Islands: Bravo Publishers, 2001.

Radio Bikini. Directed by Robert Stone. New York: IFC Films, 1987, YouTube video, 56:02, posted by Conrad Ziegfried, June 13, 2011. Accessed June 26, 2013. http://www.youtube.com/watch?v=4c14uudVDG8.

Robie, David. *Eyes of Fire: The Last Voyage of the Rainbow Warrior.* Philadelphia: New Society Publishers, 1987.

The Sound of Crickets at Night. Directed by Jack Niedenthal and Suzanne Chutaro. Majuro: Microwave Films of the Marshall Islands, 2012.

Takahashi T, M. J. Schoemaker, K. R. Trott, S. L. Simon, K. Fujimori, N. Nakashima, A. Fukao, and H. Saito. "The Relationship of Thyroid Cancer with Radiation Exposure from Nuclear Weapon Testing in the Marshall Islands." *Journal of Epidemiology* 13, no 2 (March 2003): 99–107.

Trinity and Beyond: The Atomic Bomb Movie. Directed by Peter Kuran. Narrated by William Shatner. Los Angeles: Visual Concept Entertainment, 1995, YouTube video, posted by Martin Nová?ek, August 9, 2012. Accessed June 26, 2013. http://www.youtube.com/watch?v=iUUTu2g3v00.

United States Joint Task Force One, comp. *Operation Crossroads, the Official Pictorial Record.* New York: W. H. Wise & Co. Publishers, 1946.

Weisgall, Jonathan M. *Operation Crossroads: The Atomic Tests at Bikini Atoll.* Annapolis, MD: Naval Institute Press, 1994.

Yamazaki, James N., and Louis B. Fleming. *Children of the Atomic Bomb: An American Physician's Memoir of Nagasaki, Hiroshima, and the Marshall Islands.* Durham, NC: Duke University Press Books, 1995.

LERNER
SOURCE

Expand learning beyond the printed book. Download free, complementary educational resources for this book from our website, www.lerneresource.com.

BOOKS

Bortz, Fred. *Meltdown!* Minneapolis: Twenty-First Century Books, 2011. This nonfiction title for young adult readers discusses the 2011 tsunami in Japan that led to a devastating nuclear accident at the Fukushima nuclear power plant in Japan.

Coerr, Eleanor. *Sadako and the Thousand Paper Cranes*. New York: G. P. Putnam's Sons, 1977. This nonfiction middle-grade book tells the story of Sadako Sasaki, a Japanese girl living in Hiroshima when it was hit by the first wartime atomic bomb. She died of leukemia in 1955 while attempting to fold one thousand paper cranes—a Japanese symbol of good luck.

Kelly, Cynthia C. *The Manhattan Project*. New York: Black Dog & Leventhal Publishers, 2009. This nonfiction book for teens and adults collects essays and articles describing how scientists of the Manhattan Project created and tested the world's first atomic bomb in 1945.

Klages, Ellen. *The Green Glass Sea*. New York: Viking, 2006. This award-winning middle-grade novel is set in 1943 Los Alamos, New Mexico, where the world's first atomic bomb was developed.

Meyers, Walter Dean. *Invasion*. New York: Scholastic Press, 2013. This young adult novel tells the story of two young recruits in World War II.

Sheinkin, Steve. *Bomb: The Race to Build—and Steal—the World's Most Dangerous Weapon*. New York: Flashpoint/Roaring Brook Press, 2012. For ages ten and up, this award-winning nonfiction book tells the story of the first atomic bomb and the subsequent theft of secret documents describing how to build it.

Takaki, Ronald. *Hiroshima: Why America Dropped the Atomic Bomb*. New York: Little, Brown & Company, 1995. For teens and adults, this nonfiction book explores the reasons that US military officials and President Harry Truman decided to drop the first wartime atomic bomb on Hiroshima, Japan.

Taylor, Theodore. *The Bomb*. San Diego: Harcourt, 1995. This young adult novel is about a teen boy on Bikini Atoll just before and during the first atomic bomb test on the island.

Wittenstein, Vicki Oransky. *For the Good of Mankind? The Shameful History of Human Medical Experimentation*. Minneapolis: Twenty-First Century Books, 2013. This nonfiction title for young adult readers investigates the history of human medical experimentation, including radiation testing on human subjects during the World War II and the Cold War eras.

FILMS

"*Able*, First Pictures Atomic Blast"
http://www.archive.org/details/1946-07-08_First_Pictures_Atomic_Blast. This is a film clip of *Able*'s detonation taken from 1946 military footage.

"*Able* Test, Original Footage"
http://www.disclose.tv/action/viewvideo/11658/Test_Able_Nuclear_Bomb_Testing__Original_footage/
This half-hour film clip also shows archival military footage of the *Able* explosion and the target array in Bikini Lagoon.

"*Baker*: Operation Crossroads, *Baker* Event"
http://wn.com/Project_Crossroads__Baker_Shot
This is a video of the *Baker* explosion taken from original 1946 military footage.

"*Baker* Test, Original Footage"
http://www.disclose.tv/action/viewvideo/11660/Test_Baker__Nuclear_Bomb
_Testing__Original_footage/
This video clip also shows *Baker*'s explosion.

"*Bravo*: Castle Bravo Explosion"
http://wn.com/Castle_Bravo_Explosion
This video features the *Bravo* explosion as shown in 1954 military film footage.

"The Lucky Dragon Incident"
http://www.youtube.com/watch?v=Kb4rjAmUHUk
High school student Lauren White prepared this award-winning documentary in 2008 as part of a school project. It tells how radioactivity contaminated the *Lucky Dragon* and what happened to the fishermen on the boat.

"Operation Castle Commander's Report"
http://archive.org/details/CastleCommandersReport1954
This video, prepared in 1954 by military personnel, shows the events surrounding *Bravo*.

"Operation Crossroads, Part I"
http://www.archive.org/details/Operatio1946
The US Navy produced this film describing the purpose and activities of Operation Crossroads.

Radio Bikini
http://www.youtube.com/watch?v=4c14uudVDG8
This Oscar-nominated documentary, directed by Robert Stone (New York: IFC Films, 1987), chronicles the eye-opening story of Bikini Atoll, the site of US atomic bomb tests in 1946 that left the island uninhabitable for forty years and exposed thousands of sailors to heavy doses of radiation. The film is also widely available for rent and for purchase.

The Sound of Crickets at Night
Directed by Jack Niedenthal and Suzanne Chutaro (Majuro: Microwave Films of the Marshall Islands, 2012), this film tells the haunting story of an elderly nuclear survivor from Bikini Atoll who summons a mysterious ancient deity to help reunite his family. The film provides insight into the tragic legacy of the US nuclear testing in the Marshall Islands and shows how it has impacted affected families through the years.

Trinity and Beyond: The Atomic Bomb Movie
http://www.youtube.com/watch?v=iUUTu2g3v00
Using jaw-dropping footage that was previously classified by the US government, this fascinating documentary compiled by special effects filmmaker and director Peter Kuran and narrated by William Shatner (Los Angeles: Visual Concept Entertainment, 1995) chronicles the development of the atomic hydrogen bomb. Highlights include an underwater detonation of

an atomic bomb designed to test the effect of the blast on ships at sea, as well as an interview with nuclear weapons developer Edward Teller. The film is also widely available for rent and for purchase.

World's Biggest Bomb, NOVA—Secrets of the Dead
http://www.pbs.org/wnet/secrets/episodes/the-world%e2%80%99s-biggest-bomb-watch-the-full-episode/863/
Produced by the Public Broadcasting System in 2011, this documentary describes the history of nuclear testing in the Marshall Islands and Russia.

WEBSITES

About Coral Reefs
http://coris.noaa.gov/about/
CoRIS, NOAA's Coral Reef Information System, provides information about the formation and biology of coral reefs.

Animals as Cold Warriors
http://www.nlm.nih.gov/exhibition/animals/atomic.html
This site for the US National Library of Medicine is maintained by the US government's National Institutes of Health. It discusses how atomic animals were used in the testing of nuclear devices.

Bikini Atoll
http://www.bikiniatoll.com/
Jack Niedenthal, author, Bikini advocate, and trust liaison for the people of Bikini, manages this site. It offers information about Bikini Atoll, including its part in the US nuclear testing program, resettlement, and status as a sports-fishing and diving site.

Nuclear Claims Tribunal, Republic of the Marshall Islands
http://nuclearclaimstribunal.com/
This site provides a great deal of information about the history of the nuclear testing in the Marshall Islands and the compensation related to the Marshallese affected by the testing.

Republic of the Marshall Islands Embassy
http://www.rmiembassyus.org/
The embassy site contains much information on the history and culture of the Marshall Islands and the years of nuclear testing there.

Trinity Atomic
http://www.cddc.vt.edu/host/atomic/atmosphr/ustests.html
This listing of US nuclear tests in the Marshall Islands, Nevada, and other locations includes information about civil defense, the effects of nuclear weapons and war, the stories of Nagasaki and Hiroshima, and *Trinity*, the first test explosion in New Mexico in 1945.

CONNIE GOLDSMITH has written fourteen nonfiction books for middle-school and upper-grade readers and has also published more than two hundred magazine articles, mostly on health topics for adults and children. This is Goldsmith's second book about American history. She read a newspaper story about a reunion of the Rongelap refugees and wanted to find out more about how the US nuclear testing program affected the Marshall Islands and their people. While writing the book, she interviewed experts on Bikini and Rongelap Atolls and accessed a wealth of original source materials including military reports, declassified government documents, and archival film footage. Goldsmith is also a registered nurse with a bachelor of science degree in nursing and a master of public administration degree in health care. Additionally, Goldsmith writes for nurses and for a regional parenting magazine in Sacramento, California, where she lives.

PHOTO ACKNOWLEDGMENTS

The images in this book are used with the permission of: © Bettmann/CORBIS, pp. 1, 43, 48, 60; Courtesy of the Los Alamos National Laboratory Archives, pp. 2, 28; Photo courtesy of National Nuclear Security Administration / Nevada Site Office, p. 4; Ed Westcott/American Museum of Science and Energy/Wikimedia Commons, p. 7; AP Photo, pp. 8, 32, 38; © Laura Westlund/Independent Picture Service, pp. 10, 40, 41; © Carl Mydans/Time & Life Pictures/ Getty Images, pp. 14, 16; © Underwood Archives/Archive Photos/Getty Images, p. 18; © Frank Scherschel/Time & Life Pictures/Getty Images, p. 21; © Keystone/Hulton Archive/ Getty Images, pp. 23, 25; © Associated Press, p. 29; © Robert Del Tredici, pp. 35, 70; © Stock Montage/Archive Photos/Getty Images, p. 36; AP Photo/Kyodo, p. 45; © Marshall Islands Journal, pp. 50, 69, 75; Hitoshi Yamada/Zuma/Newscom, p. 53; © Francis Miller//Time & Life Pictures/Getty Images, p. 54; © David Robie, p. 58; National Archives 374_ANT-18-CR-401-4, p. 62; U.S. Department of Energy, p. 64; © Jack Niedenthal/AFP/Getty Images, p. 66; © Bikini Atoll File Photo courtesy Jack Niedenthal, p. 71; Lawrence Livermore National Laboratory, p. 72.

Front jacket cover: National Archives ARC 6234446 (top); © WaterFrame/Alamy (bottom); back cover © AP Photo; jacket flaps National Archives ARC 6234452.

Main body text set in Gamma ITC Standard Medium 11/15. Typeface provided by International Typeface Corp.